HIKING
SOUTHERN NEVADA

HIKING
SOUTHERN NEVADA

Branch Whitney

HUNTINGTON PRESS
Las Vegas, Nevada

Hiking Southern Nevada

published by
Huntington Press
3687 South Procyon Avenue
Las Vegas, NV 89103
(702) 252-0655 Phone
(702) 252-0675 Fax
e-mail: books@huntingtonpress.com

ISBN 0-929712-22-6

Editor: Lynne Loomis
Cover design and photos: Jason Cox
Interior design: Maryann Guberman
All interior photos: Branch Whitney

This book is dedicated to Susan, and to the millions of hikers who want to keep our public lands free and accessible.

Acknowledgments

This book would not have been possible without the help of the following people: Howard Booth, Ed Forkos, Susan Murphy, and Eva Pollan.

Hike the Web

The companion Web site for *Hiking Southern Nevada* can be found at **www.hikinglasvegas.com.** The Web site features more than 350 pages of hiking information, updates to this book, safety tips, color photos, enhanced topo maps, and additional hikes from around the Southwest.

Hike Responsibly

This book is not intended to instruct the reader in the techniques of rock scrambling or mountaineering. Both activities are dangerous. You should not depend on any information gleaned from this book for your personal safety; your safety depends on your own judgment, based on your experience and a realistic assessment of your abilities. If you have any doubts about your ability to safely complete a hike in this book, do not attempt the hike.

♦ TABLE OF CONTENTS ♦

MT. CHARLESTON AREA ♦ 143

SOUTHERN NEVADA ADVANCED ADVENTURES ♦ 193

GLOSSARY ♦ 211

◆ INTRODUCTION ◆

In *Hiking Las Vegas*, I covered some of the best bouldering, rock scrambling, and hiking trails for Red Rock Canyon and Mt. Charleston. *Hiking Southern Nevada* includes all new hikes in both of these areas and introduces hikers to the many routes and trails in the Lake Mead Area.

Red Rock Canyon, 20 miles west of Las Vegas, is the recreational showcase of Southern Nevada. Comprising nearly 200,000 acres of multicolored sandstone, ancient limestone, canyons, mountains, washes, and waterfalls, Red Rock is an outdoor playground waiting to be explored.

Mt. Charleston (elevation 11,918) is less than a one-hour drive from the Strip. Hikes in this area range from 30-minute jaunts to all-day excursions and await anyone who enjoys clean air, spectacular views, and the serenity of the mountains.

In the winter, Lake Mead National Recreation Area boasts average temperatures in the 60s. From hot springs to mountain peaks, the Lake Mead Area is the perfect hiking destination during the winter.

Hiking Southern Nevada covers 50 hikes—23 in the Lake Mead National Recreation Area, 11 at Red Rock Canyon, 12 in the Mt. Charleston Area, and four additional hikes to nearby peaks. None of these hikes requires technical climbing abilities; however, some include class II and III climbing. If you've never hiked before or you're not in fit physical condition, don't attempt the tougher hikes. Start with the easy hikes and progress to the more difficult ones.

Hiking improves cardiovascular fitness and is an inexpensive way to enjoy the outdoors. Using *Hiking Southern Nevada* as your guide, you'll go beyond the lights, congestion, and confusion of Las Vegas to places where clean air, open spaces, and magnificent sights await you.

THE PURPOSE OF THIS BOOK

The goal of *Hiking Southern Nevada* is to help you enjoy the hikes in the Lake Mead, Red Rock, and Mt. Charleston Areas. I've rated the hikes according to three different factors: distance, elevation gain, and how easy it is to follow the trail or route. Using these three criteria, I've formulated an overall difficulty rating for each hike and also have provided explicit directions to the trailheads, photographs of the routes, and trail maps.

It's critical to follow my instructions from start (getting to the trailhead) to finish (returning to the trailhead safely). Pay particular attention to my descriptions of the hikes at Red Rock, as some of the scrambling routes are so remote that it could be days before another person comes across a stranded hiker. Since it's difficult to get lost on the established trails, the descriptions of these hikes are less detailed.

HOW THIS BOOK IS ORGANIZED

Hiking Southern Nevada is divided into three basic geographical areas: Lake Mead, Red Rock Canyon, and Mt. Charleston. Following are directions to these three areas. For the hikes to La Madre Peak, Potosi Mountain, Gass Peak, and Hayford Peak, driving directions and other pertinent information are provided at the beginning of each individual hike.

Directions to Lake Mead National Recreation Area

For the northern Lake Mead hikes: From the Mirage on Las Vegas Boulevard (the Strip), go north 1.5 miles and turn west (left) onto Sahara. In less than 1 mile, turn north (right) onto I-15. Take I-15 4 miles to Lake Mead Boulevard. Turn east (right) onto Lake Mead and drive 4.5 miles to Nellis Boulevard.

For the southern Lake Mead hikes: From the Mirage on Las Vegas Boulevard (the Strip), go north 1.5 miles and turn west (left) onto Sahara. In less than 1 mile, turn north (right) onto I-15. Take I-15 2 miles to U.S. Highway 93/95. Go south on 93/95 about 23 miles to Boulder City.

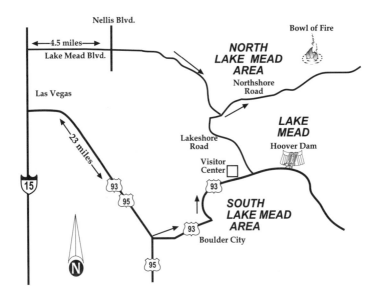

Directions to Red Rock Canyon

From the Mirage on Las Vegas Boulevard (the Strip), go north 3 miles and turn west (left) onto Charleston Boulevard. Drive 18 miles to Red Rock Canyon.

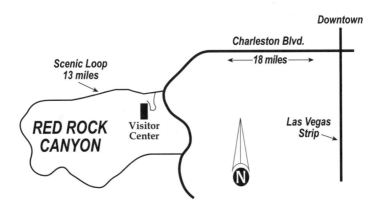

Directions to Mt. Charleston

For trailheads in the Kyle Canyon area of Mt. Charleston: From the Mirage on Las Vegas Boulevard (the Strip), go north 1.5 miles and turn west (left) onto Sahara. In less than 1 mile, turn north (right) onto I-15. Take I-15 2 miles to U.S. 95 north. Take U.S. 95 north 14 miles to State Route 157.

For trailheads in Lee Canyon: From the Mirage on Las Vegas Boulevard (the Strip), go north 1.5 miles and turn west (left) onto Sahara. In less than 1 mile, turn north (right) onto I-15. Take I-15 2 miles to U.S. 95 north. Take U.S. 95 north 27 miles to State Route 156.

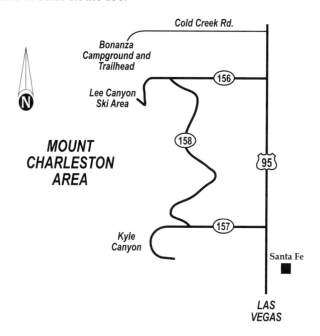

BEST SEASONS FOR HIKING

Lake Mead: Late fall, winter, and early spring
Red Rock: Fall, winter (depending on snowfall), and spring
Mt. Charleston: Late spring (depending on snowfall), summer, and early fall

FORMATS USED FOR HIKE DESCRIPTIONS

Hike: Name of the hike and type of hike (up and back, closed loop, or open loop).

Trailhead: Location of the trailhead and whether the trailhead is "marked" or "not marked" by a sign.

Distance: One way or round trip. Noted in miles.

Elevation gain: How high the trail climbs. Expressed in feet.

Elevation peak: The height of the peak. Listed only for hikes that go to peaks.

Time: The time it takes an average hiker to complete the hike.

Difficulty: Scale of 1 (easy) to 5 (very difficult). This rating is based on distance, elevation gain, and the amount of class II or class III climbing.

Danger level: Scale of 1 (safe) to 5 (use caution).

How easy to follow: Scale of 1 (well-maintained trail) to 5 (cross-country route).

Children: Designates whether it's safe for children (ages 5-11) to hike the trail with adults.

Topo map: Name of the applicable U.S. topo map.

Directions: Explicit directions to the trailhead.

Overview: Summary of the hike; also indicates whether the hike follows a trail, path, or route.

Comments: Warnings, guidelines, and interesting sights.

The Hike: Step-by-step guide to the hike.

Trails, Paths, and Routes

The hikes in this book are classified as trails, paths, routes, or combinations of the three. Let me define each to eliminate any confusion.

A **trail** is well-maintained and easy to follow. Lake Mead trails are maintained by the National Park Service. Trails are maintained by the Bureau of Land Management in Red Rock, and in the Mt. Charleston area, the U.S. Forest Service, along with the Youth Correctional Facility, maintains the trails. Official trailhead signs are provided in all three areas.

A **path** is not maintained and is difficult to follow in certain spots. Hikers usually create paths. Some paths can be heavily used—to the point where they look like trails—and others are hard to follow due to lack of use. Paths sometimes follow established trails then splinter off to different destinations. The more obscure paths use cairns to mark the way. It's easier to follow an obscure path by looking several feet ahead instead of looking down at the ground.

A **route** is hiked by using landmarks and compass bearings. No trails or paths exist. Unlike a trail or path, a route will not have obvious markings to guide you. Instead, following a route depends on locating a landmark in the distance and hiking to it. The trick with a route is to remember distinctive landmarks on your way up. Turn around often to see the view; remembering the view will make it easier to navigate the route on your return. Routes appeal to people who are adventurous and want to figure out the best way to a landmark. All of the rock-scrambling and bouldering hikes in Red Rock Canyon are routes.

Many hikes in *Hiking Southern Nevada* are combinations of trails, paths, and routes. If a trail goes over rock for a long distance, it becomes a route until the trail resumes. Many routes start from established trails. An example of a combination of the three is the Mummy Mountain hike (see *Hiking Las Vegas,* page 62). It starts on the North Loop Trail, becomes a path above Mummy Springs, and turns into a route at the chute.

Just because a hike follows a route and not a trail doesn't mean that it's easy to become lost. As an example, though all of the bouldering hikes in the canyons of Red Rock are routes, it's nearly impossible to get lost. All you have to do is turn around and hike out of the canyon.

Distance and Time

In the quick-reference feature that begins all the hikes, most of the "Distance" listings and "Time" estimates are based on a round trip for an "up and back" hike. "Closed loop" hikes start and end at the same place, so they're also assumed to be round trips. When distance is given as "one way" for an up and back or a closed loop, it's because there's much to explore along the trail, such as waterfalls or tanks. So although it might take you only an hour to do the actual round-trip trek, you could spend several more hours just looking around. "Open loops" have varying distances and times, since the main hike intersects another trail and can be done as an up and back or a loop.

Distance and time designations for open loops are based on the profile of the hike.

Danger Level

The danger-level rating takes into account the possibilities of falling, altitude sickness, and severe weather conditions. Always hike with at least one other person, and always tell someone where you're going, what trail you plan to hike, and when you expect to return.

Climbing Grades

Class I: No climbing is needed to proceed.

Class II: Hiking over rough terrain. Hands are used for balance.

Class III: Climbing requires using hands and feet. The rock is steep, though exposure is not significant.

Class IV: Climbing steep terrain. Exposure is significant and ropes are highly recommended.

Class V: Rock climbing. Technical climbing skills are a must.

Maps

Most of the scrambling and bouldering hikes don't have maps; their usefulness is minimal. However, for the hikes using trails, I've provided maps with general overviews of the hikes. Note that the maps are not drawn to scale.

Every map follows these formats:

Trail ··

Path -

Route —— —— —— —— —— —— —— —— —— ——

Paved road ━━━━━━━━━━

Gravel road ───────────

U.S. Highway (95)   State Highway (158)

Compass Bearings

All compass bearings cited in this book are magnetic north. You don't need to worry about declination. The purpose of providing compass bearings is to guide you to the correct chute, gully, or peak. The bearings set the general direction; common sense will take you the rest of the way.

CAUTIONS

The more you learn about climbing, the better prepared you'll be for the more difficult hikes covered in this book. Rock scrambling and bouldering can be dangerous, and some of the hikes in the Lake Mead, Red Rock, and Mt. Charleston areas require class III moves. Each year hikers fall and get seriously injured. Sometimes they die as a result of a fall. Again, do not hike alone. Several hikes go to very remote areas; if you fall and are injured, it may take days or weeks before another hiker finds you.

Since some of the hikes require class II and class III climbing, freedom of movement is important. Make sure your backpack isn't too restricting. In addition, a large backpack can become a hindrance, so it's a good idea to bring a rope to lower your pack to your partner.

THE 11 ESSENTIALS

All the hikes in this book are day hikes, so little is needed besides the 11 essentials. Always include the following items when preparing your backpack for a day hike: map, compass, flashlight, extra food, extra clothing, sunglasses, sunscreen, first-aid supplies, pocket knife, matches, and fire starter.

Dehydration is a serious problem. If you're not acclimated to the desert, bring twice as much water as you normally would. A minimum of a half-gallon for a four-hour hike is recommended. The old adage, "Drink before you get thirsty," is good advice. Any water found during a hike must be treated before drinking. Use a filter or tablets to purify the water.

Weather

Lake Mead is too hot for hiking in the summer. Temperatures reach 115 degrees, and very little drinkable water can be found in the area. From late fall to early spring is the best time to hike in the Lake Mead Area.

Red Rock Canyon is normally hiked from mid-September through mid-May. Temperatures in the summer months reach the 100s; if you hike Red Rock during the summer, choose the short hikes and go early in the morning. Temperatures before 9 a.m. rarely exceed 90 degrees. I've noted which hikes in Red Rock are feasible during the summer months; however, I recommend hiking in the Mt. Charleston Area in the summer.

Who said it's always sunny in Las Vegas? It is most of the time, but the "monsoon" season begins in mid-July and lasts through early September. Hikers at Mt. Charleston may start out with clear skies only to end up drenched in afternoon storms. These summer mountain storms can be very dangerous; they're often accompanied by lightning and, sometimes, hail. You don't want to be on top of a mountain in a lightning storm. During these storms, the trails become streams and your chances of being struck by lightning increase. On the day of your hike, pay attention to the weather forecast. Also try to get an early start; most storms do not kick up until past noon. Sometimes, however, storms will pass over without a drop of rain. When hiking during the monsoon season, use common sense and watch the sky for signs of stormy weather.

At Red Rock Canyon, flash flooding can also be a problem. Although it rarely rains, when it does the canyons become raging rivers. If it looks like rain, be careful. Every year people die from getting caught in flash floods. Generally, water found in the canyons is easily navigated. Standing water is normally in the creek beds of Ice Box, Pine Creek, Oak Creek, and First Creek canyons.

Getting Lost or Stuck

It's nearly impossible to get lost on the official trails at Lake Mead and Mt. Charleston. The routes in these two areas, however, are difficult to follow and should be attempted only by experienced hikers. Although it's also hard to get lost at Red Rock, it's easy to get stuck—to wind up in a place from which you can't immediately determine the way down. The sandstone terrain looks amazingly similar and there are no trails across the sandstone, so finding your way down can be confusing. But there's always a safe way down. I've tried to point out landmarks, but even with markers, it can get tricky. When you are hiking, turn around often to see what the view will look like on your return. Using rock cairns on exploratory hikes is a good idea. Some people frown on setting up cairns, but they're useful. A few cairns will help you find your way back down, and they can always be removed after you're done with them.

A stuck hiker is not in immediate danger, so asking Search and Rescue for help could possibly endanger a hiker who has fallen and really needs assistance. Call for help only if you truly need it.

I don't want to scare you, but I urge you to use caution and to follow my guidelines. Many hikes in *Hiking Southern Nevada* are easy and safe, and they follow well-marked trails. I have tried to detail a wide range of hikes. Anyone who masters the easy hikes will gain confidence and then can progress to the more difficult ones. This book includes enough advanced hikes to satisfy those people who are looking for increasing challenges.

Hiking Etiquette

Most hikers go to the mountains or desert to escape the problems of the city. Let's not bring those same problems to the wilderness areas. Always practice no-trace hiking by adhering to the following guidelines:

1. Drive and ride (mountain bikes) only on roads and trails where such travel is allowed; hike only on established trails or paths, on rock, or in washes.

2. Help keep the area clean. Pack out your trash and recycle it, pick up trash even if it's not yours, and dispose of human waste properly. Bury all human waste at least 200 feet from the trail and at least 6 inches deep.

3. Protect and conserve desert water sources. Carry your own water. Leave pools, potholes, and running water undisturbed.

4. Allow space for wildlife. Teach children not to chase animals.

5. Leave historic sites, Native American rock art, ruins, and artifacts untouched for the future. Admire rock art from a distance. Stay out of ruins and report violations.

PLANTS

Many of the plants in the Southwestern desert and mountains can be used as landmarks while hiking. By being able to identify plants and trees, you can use them as markers to retrace your steps back to the trailhead. Knowing about different plants also can aid in determining elevation and proximity to water sources. This is particularly valuable when you're hiking in Red Rock. Some common plants and trees found in the Southwestern desert and mountain areas include:

Bristlecone pine: Twisted, knotty pine, with needles in clusters of five; found at elevations of 9,000 feet and above.

Desert scrub oak: Spiny, many-branched, thicket-forming scrub; occasionally a small tree. Grows to 20 feet tall. Leaves are irregularly shaped, with sharp pointy ends that tear clothing and skin.

Juniper: A rounded tree between 15 and 30 feet tall with scale-like leaves. Produces blue-black berries.

Pinion pine: Short pine with short single needles on the twigs.

Ponderosa pine: Reaches heights of up to 100 feet. Long needles in clusters of three and lots of bark. Normally found at higher elevations, but also seen in Red Rock.

Manzanita bush: Small shrub with red-barked branches and green, non-spiny leaves.

Yucca: Clustered trunk, with sharp, thick, bayonet-like leaves 18 to 24 inches long. Flowers are white and purple.

ANIMALS

Southern Nevada boasts a variety of animal life, but except for snakes, which are rarely seen or heard, threats from animals are almost non-existent. While hiking, however, you may have the opportunity to see some of the more interesting animals that inhabit the area.

The mountain lion, also known as the cougar, puma, or panther, is the second largest North American cat. Mountain lions live up to 20 years and can weigh as much as 165 pounds. They're found around the cliffs in Red Rock and in the mountains of the Mt. Charleston Area. Mountain lions are nocturnal. If you're lucky enough to see one, don't run; cats love to chase things.

Bighorn sheep are brownish-gray with heavy horns. They are one of the desert's most adaptive animals. These animals are amazing to watch as they run straight up the mountain slopes, sometimes leaping 20 feet from cliff to cliff. Herd sizes vary depending on the time of year, but most herds contain less than a dozen sheep. Since bighorn sheep live in remote areas, their exposure to humans is limited, but they aren't afraid of people. During the hot months they stay near water sources. One of the better places to get a glimpse of bighorn sheep is deep in Oak Creek Canyon.

Pronghorn look like deer, but they're smaller with black markings on their faces. They're often mistakenly thought to be part of the antelope family. Pronghorn are between 4 and 5 feet in length and weigh from 80 to 105 pounds. Their tails are usually 3 to 6 inches long, and their black horns measure less than a foot. They're fast—able to run at speeds exceeding 40 mph. Pronghorn travel in bands of a dozen up to more than 100.

The most common large mammals found in Southern Nevada are desert mule deer. They're gray, with a darker stripe along their backs, and have black-tipped tails. Their large, wide ears resemble the ears of a mule, and this characteristic distinguishes them from other types of deer. Desert mule deer are most active late in the day, when they search for water, and at night. In Red Rock, they're often seen wandering through the thick growth along washes.

Snakes

You will seldom encounter a snake while hiking in Southern Nevada. Most snakes in the area aren't poisonous. In fact, Southern Nevada is home to only five poisonous snakes, all of which are rattlesnakes. Snakes are most active in the early morning and evening and during the months of April and October. Even though coming across a snake is rare during hikes, always pay attention to where you place your hands and feet.

VOLUNTEERING

Lake Mead:

Write to request an application from Lake Mead National Recreation Area, Coordinator Keith Eland, 601 Nevada Highway, Boulder City, NV 89005. List your areas of interest or expertise, and the coordinator will match you with a program. For more information, stop by the visitor center at Lake Mead or call either (702) 293-8990 or (702) 293-8906.

Mt. Charleston:

The contact for the following programs is Buddy Lyons at the U.S. Forest Service, (702) 873-8800.

Adopt-a-Trail Program: This is a monthly program to clean up trails; open to organizations and individuals.

Backcountry Ranger: Volunteers help patrol the high elevations during weekends and holidays. The emphasis is on trail surveys, fire prevention, and firefighting.

Campground Maintenance: Volunteers help clean up the campgrounds in the Mt. Charleston area.

Information/Education: Volunteers answer phones, provide visitor information, and assist in preparing informational literature.

Recreation Aid: Volunteers assist in the daily operation and maintenance of recreational areas.

Other:

Adopt a wild horse or burro. For more information about this program, call (702) 475-2222.

GROUP HIKING

Hike This: Offers day hikes in Red Rock Canyon. Provides packs, food, and water. For more information, call (702) 393-HIKE.

Jackson Hole Mountain Guides: Offers guided technical climbs in Red Rock. Call (702) 223-2176 for more information.

CLUBS

Las Vegas Mountaineering Club: Offers hiking and climbing outings in the Spring Mountains and beyond at skill levels ranging from beginner to advanced. The club also offers classroom and field instruction in equipment selection, map and compass use, first aid, snow climbing, and rock climbing. For more information, write to P.O. Box 36026, Las Vegas, NV 89133-6026 or call (702) 434-4323.

Sierra Club, Toiyabe Chapter: The largest and oldest hiking club in Southern Nevada. For more information, write to P.O. Box 1977, Las Vegas, NV 89132 or call (702) 363-3267.

WEB SITE

Visit my Web site at http://www.hikinglasvegas.com for more than 150 pages of hiking information, color photos, enhanced topo maps, and much more.

E-mail: branchwhitney@hikinglasvegas.com.

◆ LAKE MEAD AREA ◆

Lake Mead National Recreation Area (LMNRA) was established on October 8, 1964. It encompasses 1.5 million acres, which is twice the size of Rhode Island. The lake caters to boaters, swimmers, sunbathers, and fishermen, while the surrounding desert provides hikers with a lifetime of exploring. Three of America's four desert ecosystems—the Mojave, the Great Basin, and the Sonoran—meet in LMNRA. This seemingly barren landscape supports a surprising diversity of plants and animals, some found nowhere else in the world. Bighorn sheep, mule deer, coyotes, kit foxes, bobcats, ringtail cats, desert tortoises, numerous lizards and snakes, and a variety of birds inhabit the terrain.

For additional information about the Lake Mead Area, visit the Alan Bible Visitor Center, located four miles northeast of Boulder City, Nevada, on U.S. Highway 93. The rangers can answer your questions and provide up-to-date information on park activities and services. The visitor center has exhibits, books, brochures, and topographical maps. Located on the grounds is an outdoor botanical garden. Signs identify several trees, shrubs, and cactuses indigenous to the region.

In *Hiking Southern Nevada,* I've divided Lake Mead into northern and southern areas. The majority of the hikes, including those at the Bowl of Fire, are in the northern section. In the southern area, three of the seven hikes are in Arizona. If you do the Arizona hikes, you'll cross Hoover Dam to get to the trailheads.

The dam, situated at the southern end of Lake Mead, is a testimony to man's ability to construct monolithic projects in

FAST FACTS—LAKE MEAD

Location: 15 miles east of Las Vegas.
Directions: Northern area—Lake Mead Boulevard (NV 147), not Lake Mead Drive, to Northshore Road. Turn left on Northshore Road. Southern area—U.S. 93/95 to Boulder City. Make a left at the second stoplight onto U.S. 93 south (also called the truck route).
Visitor Center: Open daily from 8:30 a.m. to 4:30 p.m., (702) 293-8990 or (702) 293-8906.
Fee: None for hiking.
Permits: None needed for day hiking.
Camping: All six marinas. Park Service campsites are $10 per night.
Elevation range: 1,211 feet to 5,639 feet.
Size: 1.5 million acres.
Hikes: Less than 1 mile to 10 miles. Easy to moderate.
Dogs: Must be on a leash.
Horses: Yes, but poor terrain for horseback riding.
Bikes: Allowed on paved roads.
Mountain bikes: Designated trails.
Firearms: No loaded firearms permitted.
Gasoline: Available in Boulder City.
Food: Available at every marina.
Marinas: Boulder Beach, Las Vegas Wash, Callville Bay, Echo Bay, Overton Beach, and Temple Bar.
Managed by: National Park Service.

the midst of harsh conditions. Thousands of men brought their families to Black Canyon during the Depression, and these men built the largest dam of its time. It was completed in less than five years. A world-renowned structure, Hoover Dam has been rated by the American Society of Civil Engineers as one of America's Seven Modern Civil Engineering Wonders.

The Hoover Dam Visitors Center is open from 8 a.m. to 6 p.m. every day of the year except Thanksgiving and Christmas. A 25-minute historic film about the construction of Hoover

Dam is shown throughout the day, and guided tours of the dam and power plant are given from 8:35 a.m. to 5:15 p.m.

Directions to Lake Mead National Recreation Area

For the northern Lake Mead hikes: From the Mirage on Las Vegas Boulevard (the Strip), go north 1.5 miles and turn west (left) onto Sahara. In less than 1 mile, turn north (right) onto I-15. Take I-15 4 miles to Lake Mead Boulevard. Turn east (right) onto Lake Mead and drive 4.5 miles to Nellis Boulevard.

For the southern Lake Mead hikes: From the Mirage on Las Vegas Boulevard (the Strip), go north 1.5 miles and turn west (left) onto Sahara. In less than 1 mile, turn north (right) onto I-15. Take I-15 2 miles to U.S. Highway 93/95. Go south on 93/95 about 23 miles to Boulder City.

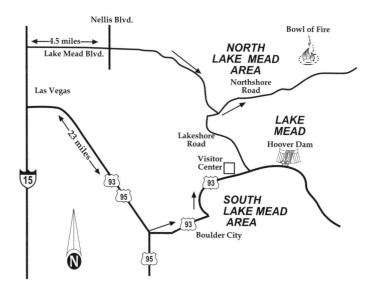

Valley of Fire

Valley of Fire, Nevada's oldest state park, is 55 miles north-east of Las Vegas. Although Valley of Fire falls outside of the Lake Mead National Recreation Area, I have included the park in this section due to its proximity to Lake Mead.

At Valley of Fire the red sandstone is set ablaze by the early morning and late afternoon sun. This 600-million-year-old sandstone has been formed into incredible shapes. Valley of Fire is more a sightseeing destination than a hiking area: Elephant Rock, Seven Sisters, and the petrified logs are breathtaking sights that can be viewed with little or no walking.

The four hikes I have included take you to parts of the park you can't see from your car. If you're in decent physical shape, you can do all four hikes in a day; if not, you can do one of the hikes and admire the beauty of the park from your car. Either way, a trip to Valley of Fire is not soon forgotten.

The visitor center, located along the Scenic Loop Road, is open daily from 8:30 a.m. to 4:30 p.m. Near the west entrance to the park, you'll find two campgrounds with 51 units. There's a $5-per-car entrance fee to the park.

VALLEY OF FIRE

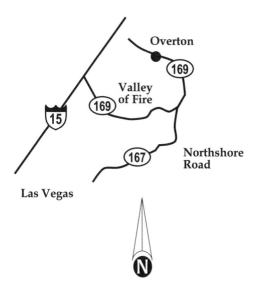

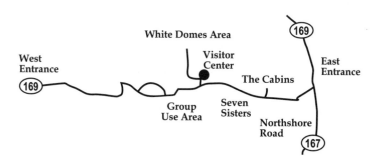

Close-up Valley of Fire

Difficulty Index

The "Difficulty Index" that follows will help you determine which hikes are best suited for your level of experience. If you're a first-timer, choose from the "Easy" category. If you have some experience (or you're a physically fit first-timer seeking more than an entry-level challenge), check out the "Moderate" category. Experienced hikers can go right to the "Advanced" hikes.

Similar charts for Red Rock Canyon and the Mt. Charleston Area can be found on pages 100 and 145 respectively. The hikes to La Madre Peak, Potosi Mountain, Gass Peak, and Hayford Peak are all advanced and should be undertaken by experienced hikers only.

Difficulty Index: Lake Mead — 23 hikes

Easy	Moderate	Advanced
Anniversary Narrows: p. 33	Anniversary Narrows: p. 33	None
Atlatl Rock: p. 67	Arizona Hot Springs: p. 91	
Callville Trail: p. 31	Dry Falls Loop: p. 74	
Historic Railroad	Fortification Hill: p. 83	
Trail: p. 78	Frenchman Mountain: p. 21	
Mouse's Tank: p. 66	Gold Strike Canyon	
Northshore Summit: p. 44	Hot Springs: p. 80	
Rainbow Gardens: p. 28	Hamblin Mountain: p. 38	
Redstone Trail: p. 50	Lava Butte: p. 25	
White Domes East: p. 69	Liberty Bell Arch: p. 86	
White Domes West: p. 71	Murphy's Peak: p. 52	
	North Bowl of Fire: p. 61	
	Northshore Peak: p. 46	
	Red Mountain and	
	Black Mountain: p. 72	
	South Bowl of Fire: p. 56	

♦ ♦ ♦

Frenchman Mountain

Hike: Frenchman Mountain — up and back
Trailhead: End of Bonanza Road — not marked
Distance: 4 miles — round trip
Elevation gain: 2,072 feet
Elevation peak: 4,052 feet
Time: 3 to 4 hours
Difficulty: 3
Danger level: 4
How easy to follow: 4
Children: no
Topo map: Frenchman Mtn., NEV

Directions: From Lake Mead and Nellis boulevards, drive 2 miles east on Lake Mead. Turn south (right) on Hollywood Boulevard and drive 1.5 miles. Turn left on Bonanza Road, drive 0.6 of a mile, and park at the dirt lot at the end of Bonanza Road.

Overview: The **path/route** follows an eastward ridge to the top.

Comments: This is one of the more aggressive routes to the peak. Frenchman Mountain looms over Las Vegas. (See Photo 1.) Many locals mistakenly believe this is Sunrise Mountain. Actually, the 3,364-foot Sunrise Mountain lies to the north on the other side of Lake Mead Boulevard.

The Hike: The unmarked trail, which is really a gravel road, starts at the far (east) end of the dirt lot. The road travels north with a slight incline. After 0.2 of a mile, the road curves to the east (right) and a path branches off the right. Look for the boul-

Peak

Photo 1

ders in Photo 2 to locate the path. Within a few yards the path becomes more defined and heads SE. The path periodically uses switchbacks to climb the steep slope.

Hike 200 yards and turn right on a path (careful—it's easy to miss!) that heads toward a rock wall. If you reach the end of the main path, you've missed the turnoff for the other path. Go back 50 yards to locate its entrance. The new path divides in 30 yards. Take either fork; they reunite in 50 yards. The path climbs a slope to a flat area. Look to the right for the continuation of the path. After a few switchbacks, the path levels again, heads north, then descends and crosses a small wash. Keep following the path until it comes to a major wash. At this point you can either head NE up the class II wash or follow the path across the wash and up the ridge. The wash is recommended, as it's more direct and easier to follow; the path is difficult to negotiate because of the loose gravel.

At the top of the wash, turn north (left) onto the original path and follow it 50 yards to a saddle. The array of communication equipment at the peak is visible from the saddle. (See Photo 3.) From this point the path becomes harder to follow; however, eventually you'll climb along the crest of a ridge. The direction of travel is obvious. You'll climb two low-angled

Photo 2

Photo 3

walls as you head NE along a faint path. Photo 4 shows the last obstacle. Climb the class III face or go left and traverse the class II terrain. Either way, you're on the ridge with drop-offs on both sides.

Photo 5 was taken from the point in Photo 4 and shows the route to the top. Just below the ridgeline, a wash begins, which provides better footing than the rocky slope. At the top

Photo 4

Photo 5

of the wash, follow a path north (left) to the collection of communication equipment. No cairn or sign-in book exists. The peak offers a stark contrast: To the west are the congestion, smog, and traffic of Las Vegas; to the east, the tranquility, solitude, and beauty of Lake Mead and the surrounding mountains.

To Descend: Retrace your steps by following the path south to the wash. At the bottom of the wash veer right toward the saddle. Descend along the ridge. You'll see the beginning of the path as it cuts across the slope about 1,000 feet below. Head toward the path.

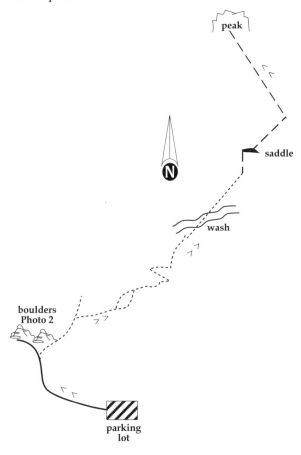

◆ ◆ ◆

Lava Butte

Hike: Lava Butte — up and back
Trailhead: Along a gravel road — not marked
Distance: 2 miles — round trip
Elevation gain: 991 feet
Elevation peak: 2,871 feet
Time: 2 hours
Difficulty: 2
Danger level: 2
How easy to follow: 2
Children: yes
Topo map: Frenchman Mtn., NEV

Directions: From the intersection of Lake Mead and Nellis boulevards, take Lake Mead 8.9 miles and turn right on an unnamed gravel road across from a sign that reads, "Lake Mead Remediation Area." Drive 0.8 miles and turn left at the fork. Drive 0.7 (1.5 total) miles and make a left. Drive 0.2 (1.7 total) miles and make a right onto another gravel road that heads toward Lava Butte. Drive 1.2 (2.9 total) miles, make a left, and drive less than 0.1 (3.0 total) of a mile. Park at the electric towers. Photo 1 is a picture of Lava Butte from Northshore Road.

Overview: The **route** travels east to a saddle, then south to the peak.

Comments: A great workout with one of the best views of Lake Mead.

The Hike: From the trailhead hike SE to the saddle (just south of point 2010 on topo) seen in Photo 2. A path develops on the

Photo 1

right side of a wash as you hike up the slope to the saddle. Once at the saddle, head south toward the peak. (See Photo 3.) It's easiest to stay along the top of the ridge. The climb to the peak is short, but fairly strenuous. The volcanic rock provides a decent surface for hiking. There's no trail or path, but the direction of travel is obvious.

The peak offers a great view of Lake Mead. Las Vegas lies SW, Mt. Charleston is west, and the Muddy Mountains are NE. There's no sign-in book at the peak.

To Descend: Retrace your steps.

Photo 2

Photo 3

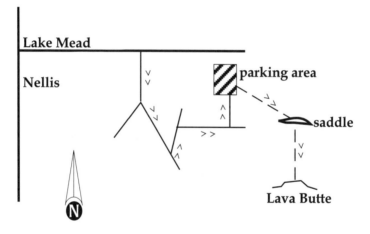

♦ ♦ ♦

Rainbow Gardens

Hike: Rainbow Gardens — up and back
Trailhead: Along Northshore Road — not marked
Distance: 5 miles — round trip
Elevation gain: 300 feet
Elevation peak: none
Time: 3 to 4 hours
Difficulty: 2
Danger level: 2
How easy to follow: 3
Children: yes
Topo map: Frenchman Mtn., NEV

Directions: From the intersection of Lake Mead and Nellis boulevards, head east about 13 miles on Lake Mead until it dead-ends into Northshore Road. Turn right onto Northshore Road and drive about a mile to a large pullout on the right side of the road.

Overview: The **route** follows a wash that heads toward Lava Butte. Follow an abandoned road south across the desert, drop into another wash, and go east to a channel of water.

Comments: You get a great view of Lava Butte and an appreciation for the diversity of colors near Lake Mead.

The Hike: The hike begins in Lava Butte Wash SW of the pullout. Follow the wash as it snakes toward Lava Butte. (See Photo 1.) The wash remains wide and the terrain has a slight incline, making this part of the hike enjoyable for all. Eventually, the wash narrows as it heads SW (220 degrees). Just past this point, it curves to the right. Instead of following the wash, continue straight onto an abandoned road. Take the road up an incline (40 yards) to a large flat area. Follow the road's faint outline as it sweeps to the right and heads

Photo 1

west (300 degrees) toward Lava Butte. In about 60 yards the road divides; take the left fork and continue south across the desert. In about a quarter-mile the road ends at a wash. Go left into the wash. You'll soon reach a section of layered dry mud that has formed into amazing patterns. The wash turns into a slot canyon with 40-foot-high walls. Along this section, another slot canyon comes in from the right, which ends at a grotto in about 50 yards. It makes an interesting side trip.

Continue as the wash curves to the right. It intersects a wide wash. You can see a dirt road climbing a hill on the far

Photo 2

side of the wash. Use the road as a landmark when you come back. Go NE (left) into the wide wash. In a few hundred yards, you'll see a mound of dirt in the middle of the wash. On top of the mound is a round pipe. If you want to hear an unbelievable echo, open the lid on the pipe and yell.

A dirt road merges with the wash. Hike along the road. When the road curves to the left and goes up a hill, veer right and continue along the wash. After 50 yards you'll come to a large channel of water, an outlet of Lake Mead. This is a great place to stop for lunch.

To Return: Retrace your steps. When you come to the second dirt road, turn right into the wash and walk until you reach the wash with the mound in Photo 2. Go left into the wash. This is the same wash you hiked in earlier. Continue to the section of layered dry mud. At the mud hike up the road that heads north (right) up a small hill. Then the terrain flattens and the road becomes harder to follow. Keep heading north about 100 yards until you intersect another dirt road. This is the first road you hiked. Go right on this road until it descends into the wash. Follow the wash back to your car.

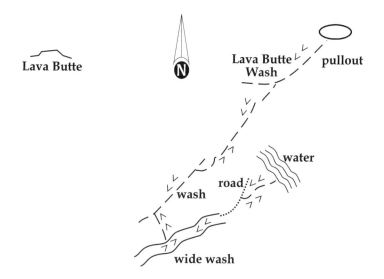

♦ ♦ ♦

Callville Trail

Hike: Callville Trail — up and back
Trailhead: Along Callville access road — marked
Distance: half a mile — round trip
Elevation gain: 200 feet
Elevation peak: none
Time: 20 minutes
Difficulty: 1
Danger level: 1
How easy to follow: 1
Children: yes
Topo map: Callville Bay, NEV

Directions: From the intersection of Lake Mead and Nellis boulevards, head east on Lake Mead about 13 miles until it dead-ends into Northshore Road. Go left, drive 7 miles, and make a right onto the signed Callville access road. Drive almost 4 miles until you see a 15 mph speed-limit sign and a sign that reads, "7 Day Limit." The trail starts just behind these signs. Continue down the road another 75 yards and park in the marina parking lot. Walk across the road to the trailhead; it's marked by a small plaque on a stand.

Overview: The **trail** heads SE to a couple of overlooks.

Comments: A good outing to introduce children and dogs to hiking.

The Hike: Follow the trail SE up the hill. The trail forks; the right fork takes you to the first overlook, and the left fork takes you to the second overlook. Both offer good views of Fortification Hill, Boulder Basin, Hemenway Valley, and the River Mountains to the south. Callville Bay lies to the north.

To Descend: Retrace your steps.

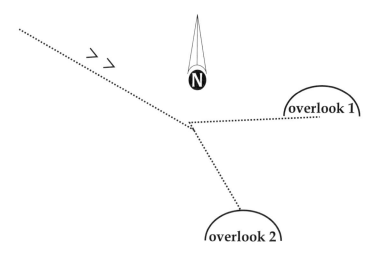

♦ ♦ ♦

Anniversary Narrows

Hike: Anniversary Narrows — up and back or closed loop
Trailhead: Along Callville Wash North Road — not marked
Distance: 4 or 7 miles — round trip
Elevation gain: less than 100 feet or 1,384 feet
Elevation peak: none or 3,073 feet
Time: 2 or 5 hours
Difficulty: 1 or 3
Danger level: 1 or 3
How easy to follow: 1 or 4
Children: yes — no
Topo map: Callville Bay, NEV-ARIZ

Directions: From the intersection of Lake Mead and Nellis boulevards, head east on Lake Mead about 13 miles until it dead-ends into Northshore Road. Go left, drive 13 miles, and make a left onto the signed Callville Wash North Road. Drive 0.2 of a mile and park at the fork.

Overview: The **trail** follows an abandoned road to Lovell Wash. The **route** follows the wash as it heads north into the narrows.

Comments: The narrows must be seen to be believed. It's a miracle of nature. If you decide to make a loop out of the hike, seeing the Bowl of Fire from the saddle is one of the most dramatic sights at Lake Mead.

The Hike: Head NW along the left fork of the dirt road. When

Photo 1

you come to a three-way divide, you can stay on the road or go south (left) and follow the wash. In about a half-mile the wash meets up with the road. Around 200 yards after the wash and road meet, you'll come to a large white sign: "Welcome To Ore Car Mine." In another half-mile (1.5 miles from the trailhead) you'll reach Lovell Wash. Head north (right) into the wash. The wind and rain have carved fantastic formations into the sides of the wash. As you curve left, you see remnants of Anniversary Mine (1922-1928) on the right bank. By hiking up the bank, you can follow an old ore-car route through two short tunnels. Once past the tunnels, drop back into the wash.

About 200 yards beyond the tunnels, the wash narrows and you'll enter the locally named "Anniversary Narrows" section of the wash. It's unbelievable that thousands of years of wind and rain have carved the narrows through a mountain. At times the canyon's walls are only five feet wide, but tower 100 feet above. This is a special place. In about 150 yards the wall recedes and the wash widens again. From here, the hike becomes much more challenging. If this is your stopping point, you've hiked nearly two miles. Retrace your steps back to your car.

To make a

Photo 2

loop out of the trip, keep hiking in the wash. Your objective is to hike into a minor wash that leads out of the main wash to a saddle. In about 200 yards as the wash curves, the majestic gray Muddy Mountains appear. When the wash di-

Photo 3

vides, hike into the east (right) fork; when it curves to the right, a side wash continues straight. Stay in the main wash, but watch for this side wash. About 100 yards beyond the side wash, you'll see a large cairn to your left and a major wash coming in at a sharp angle from the left. To your right lies a minor wash. (See Photo 1.) Hike NE up the minor wash. In less than 50 yards after hiking in this wash, you should see a patch of green malachite up on the right bank. As the wash curves to the left, you can see the saddle to the east. (See Photo 2.) This is your next objective.

Leave the wash as it curves left and head NE across the desert toward the hill in Photo 3. When you're about 75 yards from the hill, head east for the saddle. To avoid walking on the cryptobiotic soil, try to stay in any of the numerous small washes. You'll soon cross a deep wash. At the bottom, a minor wash heads east and provides an easy way to climb out of the deep wash. If you're in the correct spot, you should see a green patch of malachite about 50 yards to your north.

Wash

Photo 4

At this point the saddle is less than 200 yards away. You want to stay south (right) of the ridge that appears to travel up to the

Murphy's Peak

Photo 5

saddle, but doesn't. Hike SE to a boulder-filled wash that leads to the saddle. The wash is a strenuous class II climb. Once at the saddle, you'll come to one of the most spectacular sights at Lake Mead: You'll be looking hundreds of feet down into the Bowl of Fire. If you've never seen it, it looks like a miniature Red Rock Canyon. From this vista, the sandstone looks like it's on fire. What a contrast from the gray desert you've just hiked through.

From here, the idea is to follow a path that leads to an unnamed peak (point 937 on the topo). Start hiking south (right) along the path as it heads up a ridgeline. When the path fades, stay on the ridgeline and follow it to the peak, marked by a stake and wire. No cairn or sign-in book is present, but the peak offers a great panoramic view.

From the peak you will descend into the Bowl of Fire and out to Callville Wash North Road, where your car is parked. Hike 100 yards south down into the wash that lies between the butte and the hill. (See Photo 4.) The wash is mostly class I with a few sections of class II. It has a 20-foot drop at the end. To avoid the drop, backtrack about 30 yards and go east down into the Bowl of Fire. Head SE, aiming to the left of the red sandstone mound. (See Photo 5.) Follow the wash SE until it comes to a narrow 30-foot drop-off. Backtrack another 20 yards and head SE (same direction) up the rise. From the rise you can see Callville Wash North Road and Lake Mead. The rock changes from sandstone to conglomerate. Descend the south side of the class III slope and stay in the wash.

Once down, head south (right) in the wash until the gray ridgeline on the far side of the wash recedes. Once past the ridgeline, hike SE across the desert to Callville Wash North Road. When you reach the road, head SW (right). It's a little less than a mile to your car.

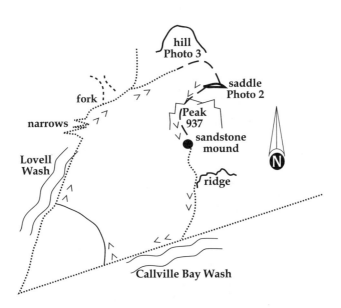

◆ ◆ ◆

Hamblin Mountain

Hike: Hamblin Mountain — closed loop
Trailhead: Pullout just past mile marker 18 on Northshore Road — not marked
Distance: 6 miles — round trip
Elevation gain: 1,440 feet
Elevation peak: 3,310 feet
Time: 4 hours
Difficulty: 3
Danger level: 2
How easy to follow: 5
Children: no
Topo map: Callville Bay, NEV-ARIZ

Directions: From the intersection of Lake Mead and Nellis boulevards, head east on Lake Mead about 13 miles until it dead-ends into Northshore Road. Go left and drive 15 miles to a small pullout a little past mile marker 18. The unmarked pullout is on the left side of the road.

Overview: The **route** heads SW in a wash before following the connecting ridgelines to the peak.

Comments: Vistas of Pinto Valley, Lake Mead, Bowl of Fire, and Las Vegas make this one of the more scenic hikes in the Lake Mead Area.

The Hike: The key to the first part of the hike involves finding the correct SW wash, which branches from locally named "Cottonwood Wash." Begin by walking 0.1 of a mile west along Northshore Road, dropping into Cottonwood Wash, and hik-

Photo 1

ing SE toward Lake Mead. You'll eventually go through a narrows lined with bedrock. When you've hiked about a mile, you'll reach Cottonwood Springs. Continue in the wash past the cottonwood trees and climb a class II half-limestone, half-sandstone wall.

Stay in the main wash when a large wash branches off to the left. You'll hike through a second narrows lined with bedrock. The wash heads east and starts to pass to the right of a ridge with patches of red sandstone and huge boulders scattered around its north slope. When the wash starts to snake, keep an eye out for the SW-heading wash. It comes in from the right. (See Photo 1.) You've hiked about 1.5 miles when you reach the SW wash.

Head SW (right) into the smaller SW wash. After roughly 75 yards, you'll pass two chocolate-colored pinnacles on your right (circled in Photo 1). Just past the pinnacles the wash bends left. Continue another 50 yards in the wash to a fork. Hike into the right fork. You'll see a red-colored bank up ahead about 100 yards. The wash you're in stays about 40 yards to the left of the red bank, then divides about 75 yards beyond the bank; hike into the right fork. The wash fades and the grade increases as

you hike south (200 degrees) through the desert. Look for a faint path that leads into a shallow undefined wash. In 100 yards the wash becomes more defined, and you'll climb a 3-foot-high dry fall. The wash turns eastward and

Photo 2

you'll climb another dry fall in 75 yards.

Once past the fall, climb out of the wash onto its right bank. From here, you'll hike along a series of connecting ridgelines to the peak. Photo 2 shows the first ridgeline you'll hike along. Go

Photo 3

SE up the slope 100 yards toward the ridgeline. When you come to a deep ravine, head south (right) about 75 yards up the steep slope. This is easier than negotiating the ravine. Once at the top, descend the far side of the slope and begin your trek on the path up the steep slope to the point in Photo 2. To your left sits picturesque Pinto Valley, and behind it is the Overton Arm of Lake Mead. At the top of the point it becomes obvious that you're on a ridgeline, which you'll follow to Hamblin Mountain. Photo 3 (taken from the point) shows the ridgelines leading to Hamblin Mountain.

Head SE along a faint path, staying along the top of the ridge. The path skirts a precarious slope as it passes left of a

Photo 4

Photo 5

knob. Hike along the top of the ridge as it curves SW (right). The ridge flattens out and offers a great view of Lake Mead. Occasionally, the path veers off the ridge, cutting across slopes. Stay up on the ridge. You'll come to a small saddle, then the obvious saddle in Photo 4. From the obvious saddle you can see the path cutting across a slope in front of you.

Follow the path as it heads SE. It soon crosses a small rockslide area and climbs to a ridge. Lake Mead comes into view again at the ridge. Head SW (right) and follow the path 60 yards to the *final* saddle. From here you're only 75 yards from the peak, which lies SW. (See Photo 5.) Follow the path to the peak.

Two wooden poles mark the peak, which offers a 360-degree view. To the NW stand the mighty Muddy Mountains; just below them lies the bright red Bowl of Fire. Las Vegas sits to the SW and beyond looms Mt. Charleston.

Photo 6

Photo 7

To Descend: You can return the way you came or make a loop out of the hike. Either way, start your descent by hiking NE back to the final saddle that lies 75 yards from the peak. From there, follow the faint path NW as it descends past the small rock-slide area to the obvious saddle. (See Photo 4.) To make a loop out of the hike, look for a greenish-tan saddle about 150 yards to the NNW. This is your next destination. To get there turn NNW (left), leaving the ridge and hiking down the slope. Follow the faint path about 50 yards, using the craggy wall for assistance. The path veers to the right and goes onto a ridgeline. If you pass two pinnacles, you've descended too far down the slope.

Once on the ridgeline, you'll see that you're west of the ridgeline you hiked up. Hike 100 yards NW down the wide ridge to the greenish-tan saddle, then look for the brownish-green pinnacle below to the north. (See Photo 6.) Head north (right) down into a small dry wash toward the pinnacle. Hike to the right of the pinnacle and follow the wash as it curves to the left and becomes rocky. Descend the class II fall and continue in the wash, which becomes defined and very pretty at this point. The wash continues winding north and starts to widen before it fades. Hike cross-country through the desert until you see the red sandstone of Bowl of Fire. At this point, head NE to the small ridge in the distance.

Descend the far side of the ridge into a wash and continue toward the Bowl of Fire. When the wash comes to an open area, follow a path that leads to the continuation of the wash. The wash heads for the steep-sided mountain in Photo 7. Climb down a dry fall and continue north through a narrows. The wash widens as it curves to the left and the Bowl of Fire comes back into view. When you intersect Cottonwood Wash, go north (left) and follow it to Northshore Road. Go east (right) along Northshore Road to your car.

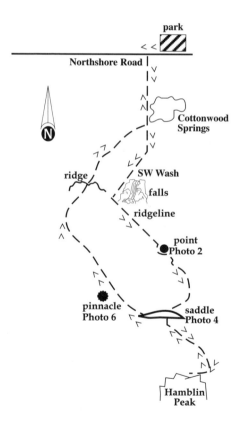

◆ ◆ ◆

Northshore Summit Trail

Hike: Northshore Summit Trail — up and back
Trailhead: Northshore Road past mile marker 20 —
marked
Distance: less than 1 mile — round trip
Elevation gain: less than 100 feet
Elevation peak: none
Time: 30 minutes
Difficulty: 1
Danger level: 1
How easy to follow: 1
Children: yes
Topo map: Boulder Canyon, NEV

Directions: From the intersection of Lake Mead and Nellis boulevards, head east on Lake Mead about 13 miles until it dead-ends into Northshore Road. Go left, drive 16 miles, and make a left into the paved parking area just past mile marker 20.

Overview: The **trail** heads west to an overlook of the Bowl of Fire.

Comments: A short hike the whole family can enjoy.

The Hike: From the signed trailhead, follow the trail west toward the overlook. The incline increases as the trail curves around the back of a hill. Stay on the main trail when a fork comes in from the right. The trail goes to an overlook of the Bowl of Fire, then continues beyond the conglomerate wall, which lies about 30 yards NE of the overlook. As you're heading north on the trail, a fork branches off SE (right). (You'll take this fork when you return.) Just after the fork, the trail divides. Take either fork; they meet up in about 100 yards along the ridgeline.

To Descend: Follow either fork back, taking a left at the SE fork. Follow this fork of the trail and make a left when it intersects the main trail. At this point you can see your car.

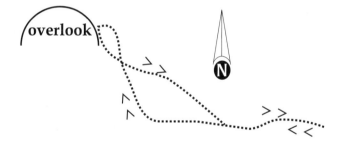

◆ ◆ ◆

Northshore Peak

Hike: Northshore Peak and knife-edge ridge — closed loop
Trailhead: Along Northshore Road — not marked
Distance: 4 miles — round trip
Elevation gain: 1,033 feet
Elevation peak: 3,329 feet
Time: 3 hours
Difficulty: 3
Danger level: 3
How easy to follow: 3
Children: no
Topo map: Callville Bay, NEV-ARIZ and Boulder Canyon, NEV

Directions: From the intersection of Lake Mead and Nellis boulevards, head east on Lake Mead about 13 miles until it dead-ends into Northshore Road. Go left, drive 0.3 of a mile past mile marker 20 (a little more than 16 miles on Northshore Road), and park along the shoulder.

Overview: The **route** travels SW up the slope and along the ridge to Northshore Peak. (See Photo 1.) From there, it travels south to the knife-edge ridge and descends NE back to Northshore Road.

Comments: Northshore Peak is locally named. This hike is one of the better hikes at Lake Mead, but it's harder than the typical Lake Mead route.

The Hike: Head SE up the steep bank that sits along Northshore

Northshore Peak

Photo 1

Road. After 80 yards veer right and traverse the slope. In another 100 yards the terrain flattens and the route becomes obvious. You'll hike east (left), around the gully to your right, before starting your ascent to the ridge that leads to Northshore Peak. Photo 2 shows the saddle that you head for to gain the ridgeline. Head south up the steep slope aiming for the saddle. Hiking on the bedrock in the wash makes for better footing while trekking up the slope. Once you're past the saddle, veer SW (right) and continue toward the peak. The grade becomes moderate as you hike along the ridgeline in Photo 1. To the south (left) is Lake Mead; a spectacular view of the Bowl of Fire is off to the north (right).

About 75 yards before the peak, you'll have to first climb down and then up a 20-foot drop. Once back up, it's easy going to the peak. A cairn (minus a sign-in book) marks the peak (1015 on the topo map). The summit offers great vistas of the Bowl of Fire and the Muddy Mountains to the north, Lake Mead to the south, and the Spring Mountains to the west.

OK, it's decision time. You can retrace your steps back to your car or continue south about a half-mile up the knife-edge ridge to an unnamed peak. Start by continuing south down the ridgeline to the saddle. Though scarier, staying next to the west (right) edge provides better footing as you descend to the saddle.

Saddle

Photo 2

Photo 3 was taken from the saddle and shows the knife-edge ridgeline. Follow a big-horn sheep path to the knife-edge ridge. Take your time climbing up the class III ridge. Once up, continue to a cairn that marks the peak (952 on the topo map).

Photo 3

To make a loop out of the hike, descend south along the ridge to a point where you feel comfortable climbing down the right side to the greenish-tan saddle between the ridge and the brown-colored mountain. Once you get off the ridge, hike north to the saddle. From the saddle you'll see part of the Bowl of Fire and a peak (point 876 on the topo map) that lies NNW. Hike north down the slope or wash, veer to the east, and pick up the path along the west slope of the ridge you just climbed. The path takes you to the east (right) of the peak to a saddle. From the saddle, follow the wash that heads north to Northshore Road. Once you get to the road, go east (right) 0.9 of a mile to your car.

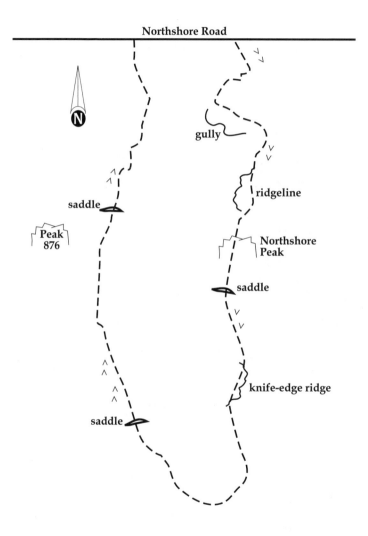

Northshore Road

N

gully

saddle

Peak
876

ridgeline

Northshore
Peak

saddle

saddle

knife-edge ridge

saddle

◆ ◆ ◆

Redstone Trail

Hike: Redstone Trail — closed loop
Trailhead: Redstone Dunes mile marker 27 on Northshore Road — marked
Distance: half a mile — round trip
Elevation gain: less than 50 feet
Elevation peak: none
Time: 20 minutes
Difficulty: 1
Danger level: 1
How easy to follow: 1
Children: yes
Topo map: Middle Point, NEV

Directions: From the intersection of Lake Mead and Nellis boulevards, head east on Lake Mead about 13 miles until it dead-ends into Northshore Road. Go left, drive 23 miles, and make a right into Redstone Dunes.

Overview: The **trail** makes a loop around the sandstone monoliths.

Comments: A number of informative plaques are found along the trail.

The Hike: The unmarked trail begins near the picnic tables along the east side of the parking area, heads SE, and soon passes the first plaque. The trail then makes a wide loop, curving west behind the red sandstone monoliths, before heading north and ending at the parking lot.

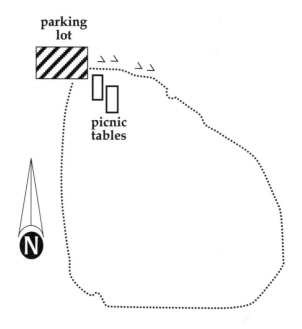

♦ ♦ ♦

Murphy's Peak

Hike: Murphy's Peak — up and back
Trailhead: Small pullout along Northshore Road — not marked
Distance: 3 miles — round trip
Elevation gain: 826 feet
Elevation peak: 2,696 feet
Time: 2 hours
Difficulty: 3
Danger level: 3
How easy to follow: 3
Children: no
Topo map: Callville Bay, NEV-ARIZ

Directions: From the intersection of Lake Mead and Nellis boulevards, head east on Lake Mead about 13 miles until it dead-ends into Northshore Road. Go left and drive 14.7 miles to a small pullout on the right side of the road. If you pass mile marker 18, you've gone too far.

Overview: The **route** cuts across the desert to a dry wash. Follow the wash up the slope to a saddle, then scramble up the east slope to the peak.

Comments: This is a quick hike with lots of scrambling. Locally named, Murphy's Peak is point 822 on the Callville Bay, NEV-ARIZ topo map. (See Photo 1.)

The Hike: Head NW across the desert. In a half-mile you'll cross Callville Bay Wash. Look for the boulder-filled wash in Photo 2; it's on the far side of Callville Bay Wash. Scramble up

Photo 1

the wash till it levels out in about 75 yards. Stay to the right of a huge four-foot cairn and head north up the slope. Scramble up a wash that starts along the slope. (See Photo 3.) When you come to the jagged wall in Photo 3, head west (left), scrambling diagonally up the ledges. Once above the ledges, the terrain flattens and you'll arrive at the first saddle.

Photo 4 shows the route from the saddle to the ridge that leads to the peak. You'll climb to the right of the crest up the ridgeline. From the first saddle head NW down to the more prominent second saddle in Photo 4. Stay along the ridgeline, avoiding the almost sheer drop-off on the right side. Once the slope becomes gentler, scramble to the right of the craggy ridgeline and make your way to the top.

Your overall direction is NW. There isn't a single route to the top, so you can avoid climbing most of the

Photo 2

class III sections. Once you're along the ridgeline, the peak lies less than 60 yards away to the north. There's no register at the peak, but the views make up for it.

To Descend: Retrace your steps to the second and first saddles; you can see them along the ridgeline. Climb down the wall, enter the wash, and cross Callville Bay Wash. Head SE a half-mile to your car.

Photo 3

Photo 4

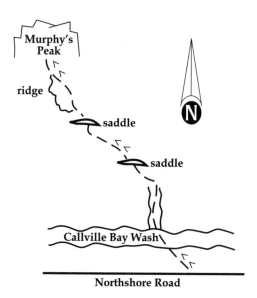

♦ ♦ ♦

South Bowl of Fire

Hike: South Bowl of Fire Loop — closed loop
Trailhead: Pullout just past mile marker 18 on Northshore Road — not marked
Distance: 5 miles — round trip
Elevation gain: 350 feet
Elevation peak: none
Time: 2 to 3 hours
Difficulty: 3
Danger level: 2
How easy to follow: 5
Children: no
Topo map: Callville Bay, NEV-ARIZ

Directions: From the intersection of Lake Mead and Nellis boulevards, head east on Lake Mead about 13 miles until it dead-ends into Northshore Road. Go left and drive 15 miles to a small pullout a little past mile marker 18. The unmarked pullout is on the left side of the road.

Overview: The route makes an elliptic loop through the South Bowl of Fire.

Comments: An adventure in a beautiful, seldom-hiked area near Lake Mead.

The Hike: Start hiking NW through the desert toward a small brown hill about 200 yards ahead. Although you can climb over the hill, it's easier to go around the right side of it. Once around the hill, head west toward the red sandstone. You'll soon cross Callville Bay Wash. Continue heading west toward

Photo 1

the red sandstone. (See Photo 1.)

When you see a large wash to your left, drop into it immediately so as not to miss the fork. The wash heads NW toward the red sandstone; at the fork, go left.

Up ahead, huge conglomerate boulders block the wash and mark the entrance to the Bowl of Fire. Climb to the left of the boulders, drop back into the wash, and continue in the wash as it passes between two small hills. Stay in the main wash, passing a wash that comes in from the left. In about 100 yards, the main wash empties into a large flat area with lots of vegetation. Ahead of you stands a towering wall of red sandstone.

Hike to the left side of the sloping wall, ascend a sandstone wash, and continue along the top of the wall. (See Photo 2.) Start by veering SW (left) and hiking up the moderately steep slope. At the top of the slope, head south about 75 yards and climb the sloping sandstone wall. (See Photo 3.)

Once up the wall, you'll enter a steep sandstone wash by going through a small arch along the left side. Continue NW, climbing the class III wash. The terrain flattens at the top. Continue north along the flat terrain 100 yards to another wash that lies some 75 feet below. Descend into the wash and head NW toward the gray ridgeline in the distance. When the wash divides near small mounds of sand-

Photo 2

stone, take the right fork and head north. In about 75 yards the wash intersects a larger wash. Turn right into it. If you're in the correct wash, you should see a mound of sandstone about 90 yards ahead littered with erosion holes. When a prominent

Photo 3

wash comes in from the left, follow it west toward a red sandstone wall capped by a gray limestone peak. (See Photo 4.) Continue in this class I wash as it snakes toward the peak.

The wash forks about 200 yards before the gray peak. Hike into the right fork, which heads directly for the gray peak. When you see the teetering boulder to your right (Photo 5), leave the wash and head NE, passing to the right of the boulder. You're now starting the loop back to the trailhead.

Continue NE, going into a small depression. Off to the east is a small rise; hike to it. From the rise, you want to hike down into the mini-valley. It's an easy descent. Once in the mini-valley, go south (right) to an opening between the sandstone crags. (See Photo 6.) Use the charcoal-colored peak (Murphy's Peak, see p. 53) as a landmark.

Once through the opening, stay to the left and follow the wash. After 100 yards, the wash becomes more defined. Soon it intersects another wash. Go left into this wash.

Photo 4

Photo 5

Does it look familiar? This is the same wash you hiked in earlier. As you head for the charcoal peak, another wash intersects the one you're in. Go left to make a loop out of the hike.

The left fork of the wash initially heads NE, then curves SE. When the wash intersects another wash, hike into the right fork and continue till you see the red sandstone wall you first climbed. It will be on your right. Veer to the SE (left) and hike to the conglomerate boulders that mark the entrance (now exit) to the South Bowl of Fire. Scramble past the boulders and continue in the wash. When you've walked about 50 yards past the conglomerate boulders, look straight ahead for the small gray hill, the same one you saw from the trailhead. This time you want to hike to the left of it. You can leave the wash any-

Murphy's Peak

Photo 6

time to make your cross-county trek (about 200 yards). You'll cross the Callville Bay Wash before weaving around the hill. Once around it, you'll be able to see your car and Northshore Road.

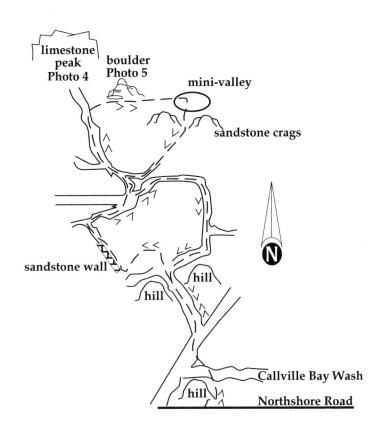

◆ ◆ ◆

North Bowl of Fire

Hike: North Bowl of Fire Loop — closed loop
Trailhead: Pullout just past mile marker 18 on Northshore Road — not marked
Distance: 6.5 miles — round trip
Elevation gain: 734 feet
Elevation peak: none
Time: 4 hours
Difficulty: 3
Danger level: 3
How easy to follow: 3
Children: no
Topo map: Callville Bay, NEV-ARIZ

Directions: From the intersection of Lake Mead and Nellis boulevards, head east on Lake Mead about 13 miles until it dead-ends into Northshore Road. Go left and drive 15 miles to a small pullout a little past mile marker 18. The unmarked pullout is on the left side of the road.

Fire Cliffs

Photo 1

Overview: The **route** heads across the desert to a wash that leads to the north side of the Bowl of Fire. Hike up a passage, then south across the top of the sandstone bluffs to the south side. Descend a wash back out through the desert to the pullout.

Comments: The Bowl of Fire is a miniature Red Rock Canyon. This route requires a compass and combines hiking through washes with some rock scrambling.

Photo 2

The Hike: Your first goal is to reach Callville Bay Wash Road. It runs SE to NW and lies about 0.7 of a mile from the pullout. Start hiking 340 degrees across the desert. You want to aim toward the left side of the red sandstone "Fire Cliffs" that lie between the gray mountains. (See Photo 1.) At Callville Bay Wash Road turn right and walk until you come to a major wash. Go left into the wash. Do not veer too far north while crossing the desert. If you do, you'll hike beyond where the wash intersects the road.

Follow this wash for almost 2 miles, until you reach the mouth of a canyon. In the first 100 yards of the wash you'll see a sign that reads, "No motor vehicle beyond this point—$500 fine." Keep in the main wash as it snakes toward the Bowl of Fire. When you come to a divide where both forks are equal, go into the right fork. The wash turns north, parallels a 50-foot-high bank, and weaves to the mouth of the canyon. (See Photo 2.)

The first part (75 yards) of the canyon is a class II scramble.

Photo 3

It then flattens out and the walls narrow. You'll come to an opening along the left wall of the canyon. Scramble to the boulders and then squeeze through the hole created by the boulders. (See Photo 3.)

Once up the hole, head SW in the wash

Photo 4

until it dead-ends into a wall about 100 yards ahead. Scramble up the left side of a low-angled sandstone wall just before the dead end. You'll be in a huge dry tank with lots of vegetation. Hike SW into a small boxed canyon. About 50 yards into the canyon on the right side is an amazing rock formation that looks like the fingers of a skeleton. You can continue up the canyon, but it's a dead end. Hike back down to the tank, then go east up the passage. (See Photo 4.)

Scramble around the left side of the boulder in Photo 4. Once past it, make a hard right and hike about 40 yards up the broken-chip sandstone to where the terrain flattens. Look down to your right and you'll see the tank and skeleton fingers.

From here, the idea is to head SW and hike about a quarter-mile to a wash that eventually leads you out of the Bowl of Fire. Start by hiking SW, and in about 60 yards you'll see whitish sandstone mounds to your far left. Veer a little to the west (right) through a wide opening with large flat boulders. Once through, the terrain opens and the sandstone turns bright red.

Photo 5

Continue heading SW toward a gray limestone mountain range. When you hike up a small rise, to your left you'll see more whitish sandstone.

At this point you can make a short side trip to the top of the Fire Cliffs. It's the perfect place to rest and eat lunch. Start the side trip by hiking SSE toward the Fire Cliffs. This is an easy class I trek that should take less than 15 minutes. The route is obvious. (See Photo 5.) The tops of the Fire Cliffs offer a great

Photo 6

view of Lake Mead and the wash you followed into the Bowl of Fire. After lunch, retrace your steps back to the point where you started the side trip.

Continue SW across the sandstone, going up a succession of small rises. Look for the circled formation in Photo 6, which marks the start of the descent. Hike just left of the formation down the slope to a large flat area covered with vegetation.

Walk SW about 75 yards along the flat area through a large opening. A sandstone mound divides the terrain ahead. Go right of the mound, descending slightly, and continue SW in a shallow wash. You'll follow the wash to a 75-foot drop-off. Backtrack about 30 yards from the drop-off to a notch in the south (left) wall of the sandstone. Use the boulder in Photo 7 as a reference. Climb down (class II) the sandstone to the wash below.

Photo 8 shows the wash as it heads west (260 degrees) and becomes more defined; you'll pass a few catch basins. When the wash turns SE, the sand gives way to gravel and a 30-foot-high bank appears on the right side of the wash. This marks the exit of the Bowl of Fire. The wash intersects the

Photo 7

main wash (the same wash you hiked to get to the east side of the Bowl of Fire) in about 1.5 miles. Head right and continue until the wash intersects Callville Bay Wash Road. You'll be able to see cars driving on Northshore Road from the intersection. If it's sunny, you'll see the glare from your car windows. Head across the desert (180 degrees) to your car.

Photo 8

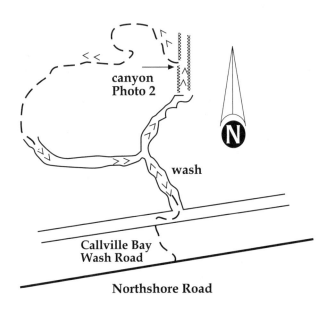

♦ ♦ ♦

Mouse's Tank

Hike: Mouse's Tank — up and back
Trailhead: Mouse's Tank parking lot — marked
Distance: 1 mile — round trip
Elevation gain: none
Elevation peak: none
Time: 20 to 30 minutes
Difficulty: 1
Danger level: 1
How easy to follow: 1
Children: yes
Topo map: Valley of Fire West, NEV

Directions: From the west entrance to the Valley of Fire, drive 3.7 miles along Scenic Loop Road and make a left onto the road that leads to the Visitor Center. Make another left onto the paved road just before the Visitor Center. Drive 1 mile and make a right into the signed parking lot for Mouse's Tank.

Overview: The **trail** heads east through Petroglyph Canyon.

Comments: The trail is named after an Indian who used the area for a hideout in the 1890s. The tank is a natural collection basin for water. The trail is also known as Petroglyph Canyon Trail.

The Hike: The paved trail begins at the east side of the parking lot by the restrooms. After 30 yards the pavement ends and you're walking through red sand. As you look ahead, you can see that you're in a boxed canyon. Go north (left) at the trail sign and walk 50 yards to Mouse's Tank.

To Return: Retrace your steps.

Atlatl Rock

Hike: Atlatl Rock Scramble — up and back
Trailhead: Atlatl Rock — marked
Distance: 1 mile — round trip
Elevation gain: 200 feet
Elevation peak: none
Time: 30 to 45 minutes
Difficulty: 2
Danger level: 2
How easy to follow: 2
Children: yes
Topo map: Valley of Fire East, NEV

Directions: From the west entrance to the Valley of Fire, drive 1.8 miles along Scenic Loop Road and make a left at the sign for Atlatl Rock. Follow the paved road to the parking lot.

Overview: The **route** travels east to an overlook.

Comments: Make sure to climb the stairs to the petroglyphs on the face of Atlatl Rock, the tallest outdoors stairs in Nevada.

The Hike: The wide trail starts at the far end of the parking lot and leads to the stairs at Atlatl Rock. After seeing the petroglyphs at the top of the stairs, continue on the same trail 40 yards past the stairs. As the trail curves to the left, veer SW (right) and follow the path that heads toward the sandstone. Photo 1 shows the sandstone crag you'll scramble up. Continue SW to the large boulders that have fallen. At this point turn left and scramble (SSE) up the steep sandstone crag to the top.

From the top you can see Lake Mead to the NE and Scenic Loop Road as it winds its way to the Visitor Center.

To Descend: Retrace your steps.

Photo 1

◆ ◆ ◆

White Domes East

Hike: White Domes East — up and back
Trailhead: White Domes parking lot — not marked
Distance: 2.5 miles — round trip
Elevation gain: none
Elevation peak: none
Time: 1 hour
Difficulty: 1
Danger level: 1
How easy to follow: 1
Children: yes
Topo map: Valley of Fire West, NEV

Directions: From the west entrance to the Valley of Fire, drive 3.7 miles along Scenic Loop Road and make a left onto the road that leads to the Visitor Center. Make another left onto the paved road just before the Visitor Center. Drive 5.6 miles and park at White Domes parking lot.

Overview: The **route** winds through a wash.

Comments: The hike passes by the remnants of an old movie set.

The Hike: The trail starts at the south end of the parking lot, goes between two huge sandstone crags, and descends into a flat area. You'll see the stone wall that was used as part of a movie set. Just beyond the wall, you'll drop into the wash. Go NE (left) in the wash. You'll go through a narrows. Once past the narrows, the wash widens. The wash then goes through a second narrows. This one is tighter and weaves more than the first. After following the wash about a half-mile, you'll reach the paved road.

To Return: Retrace your steps. Make sure to look for the old movie set. It marks your departure from the wash.

White Domes West

Hike: White Domes West — up and back
Trailhead: White Domes parking lot — marked
Distance: 1 mile — round trip
Elevation gain: none
Elevation peak: none
Time: 30 minutes
Difficulty: 1
Danger level: 1
How easy to follow: 1
Children: yes
Topo map: Valley of Fire West, NEV

Directions: From the west entrance to the Valley of Fire, drive 3.7 miles along Scenic Loop Road and make a left onto the road that leads to the Visitor Center. Make another left onto the paved road just before the Visitor Center. Drive 5.6 miles and park at White Domes parking lot.

Overview: The **route** goes through a spectacular narrows.

Comments: The temperature drops drastically in the narrows.

The Hike: The trail starts at the south end of the parking lot, goes between two huge sandstone crags, and descends into a flat area. You'll see a stone wall that was used as part of a movie set. Just beyond the wall, you drop into the wash. Go SW (right) into the wash. You'll soon go through a deep narrows. Thousands of years of exposure to the elements have created this slot canyon. Once through the narrows, you can continue another 100 yards till the wash fades.

To Return: Retrace your steps.

◆ ◆ ◆

Red Mountain and Black Mountain

Hike: Red Mountain and Black Mountain — up and back
Trailhead: River Mountain Trail System — marked
Distance: 5.6 miles — round trip, both peaks
Elevation gain: 1,065 feet
Elevation peak: 3,480 feet
Time: 3 hours
Difficulty: 2
Danger level: 1
How easy to follow: 1
Children: yes
Topo map: Boulder Beach, NEV-ARIZ and Boulder City, NEV

Directions: Take U.S. 93/95 to Boulder City. Make a left at the second stoplight onto U.S. 93 south (also called the truck route) and drive 0.7 miles to the marked River Mountain Trail parking lot on the left.

Overview: The River Mountain **Trail** heads north then intersects with the Red Mountain **Trail** and the Black Mountain **Trail.**

Comments: This is a moderate family hike with great views of Las Vegas and Lake Mead.

The Hike: The River Mountain Trail starts just behind the kiosk in the parking lot. It parallels a concrete water-retention channel for about 100 yards before heading west (left). In less than 100 yards, the trail turns westward and comes to what looks like a three-way divide. Take the left fork and continue west. The trail weaves around a hill, then proceeds toward the saddle between Red Mountain and Black Mountain. Ascend the moderate switchbacks to the saddle. There, the trail intersects Red Mountain Trail and Black Mountain Trail. Go left 0.3 miles on the Red Mountain Trail to the overlook. The trail ends at a service road. The overlook offers a good view of Las Vegas.

Retrace your steps to the intersection and head east, now on the Black Mountain Trail. Follow it a half-mile to the Black Mountain overlook. The views from here include both Lake Mead and Las Vegas. There's a bench, plus two informational plaques, at the overlook.

To Descend: Follow the Black Mountain Trail back to the intersection. Go left onto the River Mountain Trail to return to the trailhead.

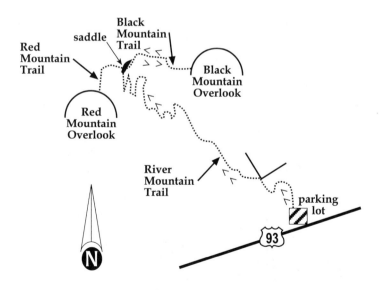

♦ ♦ ♦

Dry Falls Loop

Hike: Dry Falls Loop — closed loop
Trailhead: By the water tank — not marked
Distance: 7 miles — round trip
Elevation gain: 1,020 feet
Elevation peak: none
Time: 4 hours
Difficulty: 3
Danger level: 3
How easy to follow: 4
Children: no
Topo map: Boulder Beach, NEV-ARIZ

Directions: Take U.S. 93/95 to Boulder City. Make a left at the second stoplight onto U.S. 93 south, also called Lakeshore Road. Drive 3.5 miles and turn left onto a paved road with a "No Hunting Area" sign. (If you pass the Visitor Center, you've gone too far.) Drive 0.1 of a mile and turn left onto a gravel road just before the pumping station. In 1.5 miles the road comes to a three-way divide. Go right, drive 0.3 of a mile, and park at the huge water tank.

Overview: The **route** follows a west-traveling wash, then circles and follows an east-traveling wash.

Photo 1

Comments: The hike

offers great vistas of Lake Mead. You'll climb a total of eight dry falls and descend one during the hike. Keep an eye out for bighorn sheep!

Photo 2

The Hike: From the water tank, head west across the desert and pick up a dirt road that heads into the canyon. You'll pass an iron gate. The road swings to the right, then to the left, passing a gravel pit before turning into a wash. The canyon walls close in and the wash divides. Take the right fork. Immediately you're challenged by the first dry fall. (See Photo 1.) Continue 40 yards past the first dry fall to the second dry fall. Look for the opening that leads to the top.

Continue in the wash, watching for catclaw bushes; they easily snag clothing. As the wash heads NW, the hiking becomes easy. The third dry fall lies about 300 yards past the second. Scramble up it and continue in the wash. The fourth dry fall is only 5 feet high and a much easier climb than the first three.

Photo 3

Continue in the wash. The fifth dry fall is made up of several smaller dry falls. After climbing the first one, go to the left and climb the second. The third fall, a class IV climb, is about 15 feet high. Scramble out of the wash along the right bank to get around it. The sixth fall, which is also sheer, lies about 40 yards ahead. Stay high to get up and around it. Do the same for the seventh. Once past it, drop back into the wash. In about 100 yards you'll come to the easily navigated eighth dry fall. It's distinguish-

Photo 4

able by the pink-ish-colored rock. Hike 50 yards to a three-way divide. Head west into the right fork. The incline becomes moderate. In 250 yards, the wash divides again. Scramble into the right fork and follow it NW to a ridgeline. It's a short, but strenuous, scramble to the ridgeline. At the ridgeline, Lake Mead is visible to your east (right). Your next objective is to drop down into a wide wash, which lies NW of your current position and is not visible.

Begin by heading west along a faint path, probably made by bighorn sheep. Head toward the dark-colored peak. The wide wash lies before this peak. Photo 2 shows the dark-colored peak and the saddle you're aiming for. Stay high as you head for the saddle to avoid hiking up and down the banks of a wash.

From the saddle, you'll see the wide wash. Hike down, go NE (right), and follow it. In a few hundred yards the walls start to close in and you'll scramble down a dry fall. Take it slow; the sides are slick. About 40 yards past the dry fall, you'll leave the wash and hike up to the ridge. Photo 3 shows where to leave the wash. Look for the catclaw bush (circled in Photo 3) to help you find the correct spot. The reason you leave the wash is to avoid multiple class V dry falls.

Once you're past the catclaw bush, veer right. You'll come to a small flat area. From there, go north through the rocky pinnacles. Photo 4 shows hikers as they head NE up a slope, between a rise and a brownish wall. At the top of the slope, you'll arrive at another flat area covered with lots of reddish pebbles. A hundred yards to the east you'll see a small hill. Just before the hill, go north (left) up a low-angled wall. Head NE about 50 yards to a great vista of Lake Mead. At this point, start heading east down the slope into a wash. Follow the wash until it comes to a drop-off. Head north (left) and work your way down the slope. From here you'll see a deep wash. To drop into it, go to the NE end, which provides the easiest access. Once in the wash, follow it SE as it descends into a main wash.

At the main wash, go left and follow it to a dirt road located near the power lines. Go SE (right) onto the upper dirt road. When the road forks, go left, join up with the main road, and continue SE. You'll soon see the water tank.

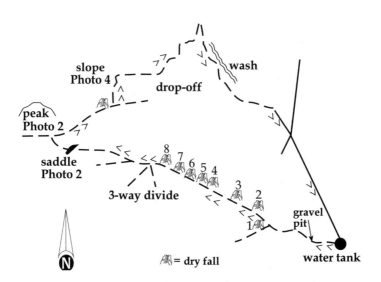

Historic Railroad Trail

Hike: Historic Railroad Trail — up and back
Trailhead: Pullout parking area across from Visitor Center — not marked
Distance: 5.2 miles — round trip
Elevation gain: less than 100 feet
Elevation peak: none
Time: 2 hours
Difficulty: 1
Danger level: 1
How easy to follow: 1
Children: yes
Topo map: Boulder Beach, NEV-ARIZ

Directions: Take U.S. 93/95 to Boulder City. Make a left at the second stoplight onto U.S. 93 south. Drive 4 miles and make a right into the parking lot across from Alan Bible Visitor Center.

Overview: The **trail** heads east, passing through four railroad tunnels.

Comments: The trail follows the right-of-way of a railroad built in 1931 to bring supplies for the construction of Hoover Dam. Part of the trail was used in the film *The Gauntlet* for a scene in which Clint Eastwood and Sondra Locke, riding a motorcycle, are being chased by a helicopter.

The Hike: The spur trail begins at the SE corner of the parking lot. It heads east and shortly joins with the real trail. Soon you'll come to a locked gate that prohibits vehicles from driving on the trail. Follow the signs around the fence. As the trail bends to the right, you get a great view of Lake Mead, which lies 100 feet below.

You'll pass through four tunnels, each approximately 300 feet long and 25 feet high. The trail ends at the fifth tunnel, which was sealed in 1978.

To Descend: Retrace your steps.

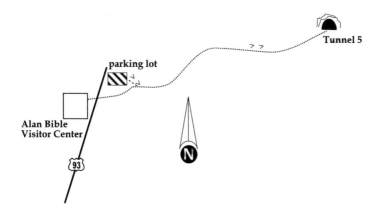

◆ ◆ ◆

Gold Strike Canyon Hot Springs

Hike: Gold Strike Canyon Hot Springs — up and back
Trailhead: Hacienda Casino — marked
Distance: 6 miles — round trip
Elevation gain: –800 feet (descent)
Elevation peak: none
Time: 2 hours (one way)
Difficulty: 3
Danger level: 5
How easy to follow: 2
Children: no
Topo map: Boulder Beach, NEV and Hoover Dam, NEV

Directions: Take U.S. 93/95 to Boulder City. Make a left at the second stoplight onto U.S. 93 south, also called Lakeshore Road. Drive 4.6 miles to the Hacienda Casino. Park at the casino.

Overview: The **route** parallels U.S. 93, drops into a wash, and heads SE to the signed trailhead. It then follows the wash through Gold Strike Canyon to the hot springs.

Comments: Because of break-ins to vehicles at the official trailhead, park at the Hacienda Casino and walk. This hike offers stunning sights. The wash travels between deep canyon walls and weaves around a waterfall. The rocks and boulders are *extremely* slippery. You'll descend eight major dry and wet falls. Although it's possible to hike to the Colorado River, the route description stops at the second pool. From there to the Colorado River is for sure-footed hikers only. There are many ways to navigate the dry and wet falls; I've explained some of the easiest. Also, look for blue arrows to guide you.

The Hike: Hike east along U.S. 93 toward Hoover Dam. At mile marker 3 (along a guardrail), a faint abandoned road starts and descends about 60 yards SE to a shallow wash. Go east (left) in the shallow wash. You'll soon come to a couple of gravel roads. The roads are marked 75 and 75A. Follow 75A east to the Gold Strike Canyon trailhead sign. This is the official parking area for the hike; as I mentioned, vehicles parked here get broken into a lot. From the casino where you parked to this point is a little more than a half-mile.

Photo 1

The wash heads east and declines gradually. Soon you'll walk between 100-foot-high canyon walls with incredible rock formations. Eventually, you'll come to the first dry fall. Follow the left path. Once past the fall, the path drops into the wash.

Photo 1 shows hikers descending the second dry fall. Use the steps chiseled into the boulder to aid your descent. The boulder is slippery, so take it nice and slow. Two down—six more falls to go!

Seventy yards past the second fall, you'll pass under telephone wires. Beyond the telephone wires, the canyon forks. Stay in the main canyon and continue in the wash.

Photo 2

When you encounter the third dry fall, go to the left and climb down. Just beyond the third fall, a path weaves through catclaw bushes.

The fourth and fifth falls are easily navigated. The sixth fall might have water, depending on the recent rainfall. Go to the right to get down it. At the seventh fall, go along the left wall of the canyon and use the log that's propped against the wall. Once down, look to your right for the first pool. The warm water and the serenity of the canyon are relaxing. This should be the stopping point for anyone having trouble negotiating the falls.

After the seventh fall, your shoes will probably get wet and make climbing tricky. You'll walk along spots where the temperature feels like it has increased 20 degrees; this kind of temperature spike is one reason to avoid this hike in the summer.

Conquering the eighth and final waterfall involves using a rope to help you descend a large boulder. Once you're down, the second pool is to your immediate right. (See Photo 2.) This pool is deeper than the first. Many hikers take off their backpacks before descending the boulder. If you're prepared and if you're an experienced hiker, you can go all the way to the Colorado River. However, I don't recommend continuing past this point because the hike becomes even more strenuous and potentially dangerous.

To Return: Retrace your steps.

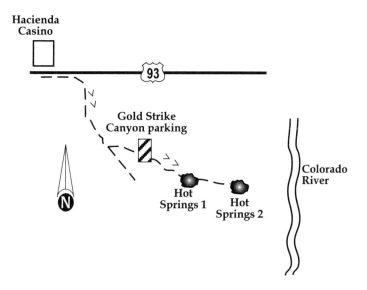

Fortification Hill

Hike: Fortification Hill — up and back
Trailhead: Along Fortification Road — marked
Distance: 6 miles — round trip
Elevation gain: 1,197 feet
Elevation peak: 3,657 feet
Time: 3 to 4 hours
Difficulty: 3
Danger level: 2
How easy to follow: 2
Children: no
Topo map: Hoover Dam, ARIZ

Directions: Take U.S. 93/95 to Boulder City. Make a left at the second stoplight onto U.S. 93 south. Drive 2.1 miles past the "Welcome to Arizona" sign at Hoover Dam and turn left on Kingman Wash Road. At 3.4 miles you'll pass an outhouse at Painter's Cove. Beyond the cove, the road is called Fortification Road. Continue another 2.7 miles and park near a small metal trailhead sign located on the north (left) side of the road. (See Photo 1.)

Overview: The **path** follows a ridge north to the summit.

Comments: The view from Fortification Hill rivals any vista around Lake Mead. On a clear day, with snow covering Mt. Charleston in the distance, an award-winning photograph awaits. A mile-long mesa lies at the top of Fortification Hill.

The Hike: Head west along the wash. In 100 yards the trail veers left; do not follow it. Instead, veer right and follow a minor wash that goes north. There's a ridge to your NE (right) that you must gain. (See Photo 2.) You can gain it immediately or parallel it waiting for the ridge to dip. Either way, once along the ridgeline, follow the path that heads NW

Fortification Hill

Photo 1

toward Fortification Hill. You'll encounter steep sections along the ridge, but they're followed by level terrain. In places where the path fades, keep heading toward the east (right) side of Fortification Hill. Eventually, you'll pass the boulders in Photo 3. From the boulders, it's about 150 yards of steep terrain to the base of the wall just below the mesa. Once at the wall, the path cuts east (right) and levels out. Hike about 100 yards and climb the wall in Photo 4. It's an easy class II climb. If the path starts descending while you're traversing, you've gone too far. At the top of the wall, the path heads north. It soon makes a hard left and uses switchbacks to climb the last few yards to the mesa.

The well-defined path heads south; it's almost a mile to the peak. This is the most enjoyable part of the hike. The last 50-yard climb to the peak is moderately steep. At the peak you'll be treated to a view that will take your breath away. To

Ridge

the west lie Lake Mead, Las Vegas, and the snow-capped peaks of Mt. Charleston. Hoover Dam sits to the SW. The rugged Muddy Mountains are to the north. The Bowl of Fire is in front of them. Be sure to sign the register inside the army box.

Photo 2

NE of the peak are remnants of a volcanic crater; it's a short hike from the peak.

To Descend: Retrace your steps.

Photo 3

Photo 4

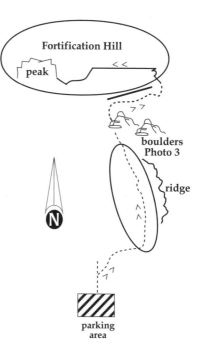

♦ ♦ ♦

Liberty Bell Arch

Hike: Liberty Bell Arch — closed loop
Trailhead: Along U.S. 93 — not marked
Distance: 5 miles — round trip
Elevation gain: 151 feet
Elevation peak: none
Time: 3 to 4 hours
Difficulty: 2
Danger level: 2
How easy to follow: 3
Children: yes
Topo map: Ringbolt Rapids, ARIZ-NEV

Directions: Take U.S. 93/95 to Boulder City. Make a left at the second stoplight onto U.S. 93 south. Drive 3.1 miles past the "Welcome to Arizona" sign at Hoover Dam and park at an unmarked gravel pullout on the left side of the road.

Overview: The **path** heads west to Liberty Bell Arch. From the arch it travels to an overlook of the Colorado River.

Comments: This is a must-do hike. Thousands of years of wind and rain have formed a spectacular arch through the conglomerate rock, and a perfect lunch spot overlooks the Colorado River. The rugged terrain and the solitude of this hike will appeal to anyone who likes the outdoors.

The Hike: The trick is to find the start of an abandoned dirt road that serves as the trailhead. From the pullout, cross the highway and walk west (right) to a guardrail, which is visible from the pullout. Walk NW along the inside of the guardrail, passing a couple of thin metal stakes. Follow a faint path that passes to the left of an aluminum drainage pipe. The path forks about 30 yards past the pipe. Go left and turn onto the abandoned road. You're now at the trailhead of a great hike.

Photo 1

In 200 yards the abandoned road forks. Go right. The path curves SE. It's easy to follow and goes toward an unnamed peak (Photo 1). At the bottom of a slope, the path passes between two large boulders, then makes a U-turn and heads SW up another slope.

The path turns west and travels up a third slope to the top of an old mine, marked by a wooden sled-like piece of mining equipment. Follow the path down the backside of the slope. As the path travels down the slope, it makes a hard right before it forks. Take the right fork, which goes to the mine. The mine, about 50 feet in length, was active in the 1940s. Photo 2 is a picture of Liberty Bell Arch taken from the mine. From this angle you can't see the arch. (The mountain in the photo serves as a landmark.)

From the mine, retrace your steps to a wash that heads south toward Liberty Bell Arch. Eventually you'll pass greenish rocks in the wash. In 80 yards, the path resumes on the wash's right bank and travels NW up a gentle slope. Near the top of the slope, the arch comes into view. (See Photo 3.)

At the top of the slope the path intersects another

Photo 2

Photo 3

path. Go SW (left) on the path as it heads toward the arch. You'll come to a high point that's less than 200 yards from the arch. The main path swings to the left; however, a faint path leads to the base of the arch. If you try climbing into the arch, you must climb a class III crack. Because the rock crumbles easily, I advise against it.

To get to the overlook, continue SW on the path as it climbs a slope. The path disappears when it goes over rocks; look for cairns if you lose the path and continue up the slope. Once the terrain flattens, the path is easy to follow. Continue south to

the wash in Photo 4. Go SE (left) down into the wash and follow it 100 yards to an awesome overlook of the Colorado River and White Rock Canyon. If it's windy, this is the best place to escape the wind and eat lunch.

When you're ready to leave the overlook,

Photo 4

hike NW in the same wash to the path. Go SW (left) on the path and follow it to another great overlook of the Colorado River. This is a perfect place for lunch if there's no wind.

To Descend: Once you've had your fill of food and views, head NE on the same path, past Liberty Bell Arch. You will arrive at the previous intersection. Go right and take the same path back, or continue north and make a loop out of the hike. If you go straight, the path is easy to follow as it traverses a

Photo 5

slope. Very soon, you can look right and see the original path. A giant cairn marks the path as it climbs over volcanic rock. Head north 100 yards to a small saddle where the path ends. Look for the peak that stands above another saddle in Photo 5.

An arrow made from rocks marks the wash. Go north

Photo 6

down the wash (class II) into another wash. Once in the wash, head east (right). Make sure you stay in the main wash, which snakes north toward the highway. When you come to a 20-foot wall, climb the class II chute on the left. Drop back down into the same wash and hike NE. The wash is filled with large boulders. Beyond the boulders, hike 40 yards in the wash, then walk up the 10-foot, sloping right wall of the wash. (See Photo 6.) At the top of the wall, another wash continues toward the highway. You'll soon see the highway and the guardrail you walked along at the start of the hike. At the guardrail you'll be able to see your car parked across the highway. Be careful crossing the highway.

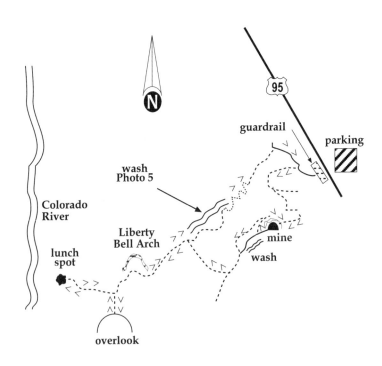

◆ ◆ ◆

Arizona Hot Springs

Hike: Arizona Hot Springs — up and back or closed loop
Trailhead: Dirt parking lot off U.S. 93 — marked
Distance: 6 miles — round trip
Elevation gain: –586 feet (descent)
Elevation peak: none
Time: 4 hours
Difficulty: 2
Danger level: 3
How easy to follow: 3
Children: no
Topo map: Ringbolt Rapids, ARIZ-NEV

Directions: Take U.S. 93/95 to Boulder City. Make a left at the second stoplight onto U.S. 93 south. Drive 3.9 miles past the "Welcome to Arizona" sign at Hoover Dam to a gravel road just past the bridge. Turn right and follow the gravel road 50 yards to the parking area.

Overview: The **route** weaves through White Rock Canyon to the Colorado River, then travels a quarter-mile to the hot springs.

Comments: If you plan to soak in the hot springs, wear your bathing suit under your clothes as there are few secluded places to change. I also recommend bringing a pair of tennis shoes to change into so your hiking boots stay dry. The hot springs produces 400 gallons of water per minute with a temperature range of 85 degrees to 120 degrees, but normally around 103 degrees. Warning: An amoeba common to thermal pools may be present.

It's been known to cause a rare infection that results in death. Do not dive into the hot springs or submerge your head.

Photo 1

The Hike: The trail begins at the sign that reads, "Lake Mead National Recreation Area — White Rock Canyon — Lake Mojave (Colorado River) 2.3 miles — Arizona Hot Springs 2.8 miles." The trail heads SW toward the Colorado River. In 100 yards take the right fork and continue toward the river. The trail curves right and drops into a sandy wash that leads through the magnificent White Rock Canyon. This twisting narrow canyon has 100-foot-high volcanic rock walls. Follow the class I wash through the canyon to the Colorado River. If you're hiking at a pace that equals at least 2 miles per hour, you should be at the river in an hour.

At the river, finding the route and traversing terrain become trickier. Your goal is to follow a trail 0.7 of a mile to a nearby canyon that leads to the hot springs. Begin by locating the dirt trail near a rock wall. The trail heads south and parallels the river. In 50 yards you'll pass a trail sign. Keep a sharp eye out for another trail sign that points to the left. Go left across the rock (no trail) and climb a low-angled wall, or walk about 30 yards toward the river where the wall is less steep. From the top of the wall you just climbed, you can see a second low-angled wall. (See Photo 1.)

Once you climb the second wall, the trail is easy to follow.

Trail sign

Photo 2

Photo 3

The trail intersects another trail at the top of a hill. Continue south on the main trail as it descends and soon drops into the canyon that leads to the hot springs. A trail sign marks this spot. (See Photo 2.) If you brought tennis shoes, put them on.

Go north (left) into the canyon and follow the wash. You'll soon encounter water flowing from the hot springs. Be careful of slippery rocks as you climb a number of wet falls. After you climb the 20-foot steel ladder, it's 50 yards to the hot springs. (See Photo 3.) Don't be surprised if others are enjoying the hot springs. After soaking, it's important to eat something; the hot water saps energy.

Once you've finished soaking, you have a decision to make: You can return the way you came or make a loop out of the hike. If you return the same way, eat lunch at a spot on the Colorado River. To hike to the Colorado River, retrace your steps, climb down the ladder, and continue past the trail sign. The river lies less than 100 yards from the trail sign. After lunch hike back up the same wash, making a left at the trail sign, and follow the same trail back to White Rock Canyon.

If you make a loop out of the hike, pass all your gear to the

Photo 4

far side of the hot springs so you don't have to climb back down to get it. If hiking to the hot springs was tough for you, return the way you hiked in. The next part of the hike is much tougher.

After soaking, hike past the hot

springs and climb up an angled wall. Once you're up, the canyon walls recede and a wide wash forms. This is a great place to have lunch. Let the wind and sun dry you off.

Photo 5

Start hiking east in the wash. You'll hike through narrow parts of the canyon and walk in wide washes. There are a few dry falls to climb, but don't be disappointed; the big ones are up ahead. If you're hiking at a 2-miles-per-hour pace, in about 30 minutes watch for a side wash on your left. Hike east in this wash. (See Photo 4.)

After 100 yards you can see a narrow canyon. Just before this spot, petroglyphs are scattered on the boulders to your left. You'll come to the first and easiest of three dry falls. Photo 5 shows the second dry fall. You can climb (class III and strenuous) this dry fall or scramble up the right side and go through a hole in the rock. The third and final dry fall is less than 100 yards away. The fall is a class IV or class V climb. To avoid this climb, backtrack about 30 yards and climb (class III) the angled wall along the left side of the canyon shown in Photo 6.

You'll soon come to a minor wash that forks right and serves as a landmark. About 30 yards past the minor wash, leave the wash you're in and follow a faint path north toward the highway. Once you're up the rise, the highway is visible in the distance. Follow

Photo 6

the path as it swings NW and heads toward White Rock Canyon. The path crosses a minor wash. From the far side of the minor wash, you'll be able to see your car in the parking lot.

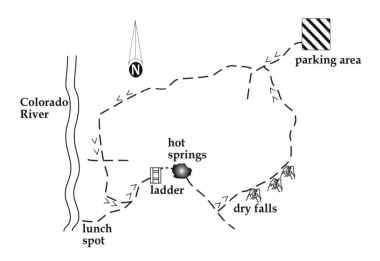

♦ RED ROCK CANYON ♦

Red Rock Canyon, 20 miles west of Las Vegas, is the recreational showcase of Southern Nevada. Comprising nearly 200,000 acres of multicolored sandstone, ancient limestone, canyons, mountains, washes, and waterfalls, Red Rock is an outdoor playground waiting to be explored. The 2,000-foot-high sandstone walls make the canyons in Red Rock unique; you can spend hours bouldering. Unlike many other sandstone mountains in the United States, the peaks at Red Rock Canyon can be climbed without using ropes. Think of Red Rock as a giant maze and this book as a cheat sheet that shows you the twists and turns around towering walls and narrow ledges.

The 11 hikes in this section range in difficulty and route-finding ability. The easy hikes follow established trails and are suitable for families, while the advanced hikes wind through canyons and up to seldom-hiked peaks. Most of the advanced hikes in this book, in my previous book *Hiking Las Vegas*, and on my Web site, I've designed, cairned, and maintained. For the latest updates and trail conditions, visit my Web site: www.hikinglasvegas.com.

Directions to Red Rock Canyon

From the Mirage on Las Vegas Boulevard (the Strip), go north 3 miles and turn west (left) onto Charleston Boulevard. Drive 18 miles to Red Rock Canyon. See map on next page.

FAST FACTS—RED ROCK CANYON

Location: 20 miles west of Las Vegas.

Directions: Drive west on Charleston Boulevard (State Route 159) and turn right into Red Rock Canyon.

Visitor Center: Open daily from 8:30 a.m. to 5 p.m., (702) 363-1921. Limited hiking information available.

Fee: $5 per car; $20 for a yearly pass. Golden Eagle Pass is accepted.

Permits: None needed for day hiking.

Camping: 13 Mile Campground, located on State Route 159 about 2 miles before the entrance to Red Rock. $10 per night. Water and toilets available.

Elevation range: 3,394 feet to 7,092 feet.

Size: 195,610 acres.

Hikes: From 1 mile to 15 miles. All ranges of difficulty.

Dogs: Must be on a leash.

Horses: Designated trails.

Bikes: Allowed on Scenic Loop.

Mountain bikes: Designated trails.

Firearms: Not permitted.

Gasoline: None available.

Food: Available at Bonnie Springs, located along State Route 159 about 5 miles beyond the turnoff for Scenic Loop.

Scenic Loop: A 13-mile *one-way* paved road that's used to get to many of the trailheads. Open from 7 a.m. to dusk.

Managed by: Bureau of Land Management, (702) 647-5000.

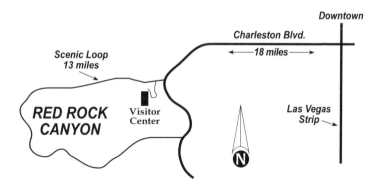

Pine Creek Map

The following map shows and names all the forks of Pine Creek and the nearby peaks in this section of Red Rock Canyon. The map is for general reference only.

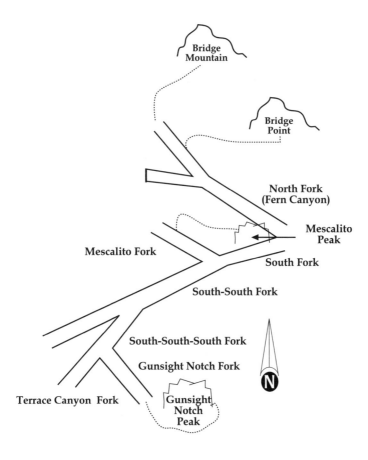

Difficulty Index: Red Rock Canyon — 11 hikes

Easy	Moderate	Advanced
Arnight Trail: p. 140 Dale's Trail: p. 138 Ice Box Canyon 　Loop: p. 136 Sandstone Quarry 　Loop: p. 116	Britt's Loop: p. 111 Calico Tank: p. 101 Calico Tank Peak: p. 104 Sandstone Quarry 　Overlook: p. 118	Gunsight Notch Peak: 　p. 129 Mescalito: p. 121 Terrace Canyon: p. 133

♦ ♦ ♦

Calico Tank

Hike: Calico Tank — up and back
Trailhead: Sandstone Quarry — marked
Distance: 2.5 miles — round trip
Elevation gain: 450 feet
Elevation peak: none
Time: 1 to 2 hours
Difficulty: 2
Danger level: 1
How easy to follow: 2
Children: yes
Topo map: La Madre Mtn., NEV

Directions: The signed pulloff for Sandstone Quarry is located 2.8 miles past the Scenic Loop gate. The marked trailhead is at the far end of the parking lot.

Overview: The **trail** heads NW and empties into a wash. The wash travels east to Calico Tank.

Comments: This is one of the most popular trails in Red Rock Canyon. Water in Calico Tank can vary from none to a depth of several feet and can even be frozen in the winter.

The Hike: Hike NW 75 yards along the signed gravel trail until it disappears into a shallow wash. Walk NW 10 yards in the wash to a point where the trail resumes. (You'll see large sandstone rocks that resemble overgrown children's blocks; stay to the left of them.) Continue to a major fork, where a trail sign indicates to go right onto the Calico Tanks Trail. Walk about 125 yards and turn right at the sign for Calico Tanks. The trail narrows to a single-track trail. Follow this trail 100 yards into a dry wash. In about 75 yards from the start of the wash, the trail leaves the wash and heads east (right). It soon drops back into a small wash. When the wash divides, go either way; the forks rejoin after 30 yards. Perched high on a sandstone crag is a distinctive boulder. (See Photo 1.) This is a key landmark that you'll head toward and eventually pass.

Photo 1

The wash is intermittently broken up by sandstone as seen in Photo 2. This is one of the few class II sections along the hike. About 40 yards beyond the scene in Photo 2, hike up sandstone stairs that begin along the south (right) side of the wash, then follow the route back into the wash. The wash stops again at chiseled steps carved in the sandstone. Once up the steps, veer left and follow the route up more sandstone stairs. (See Photo 3.)

At the top of the stairs, head SE (right) toward the wash. At the wash, the trail continues and leads to more sandstone steps along the south (right) side. At the top of the steps, the trail resumes and climbs to a high point. From this point you can see the saddle that sits about 250 yards up ahead. Just be-

yond the saddle lies Calico Tank. Follow the trail to the tank.

At the tank you can either explore or relax and take in the sights. This is a popular destination on the weekends. Calico Tank is just one of many tanks hidden throughout Calico Hills.

Photo 2

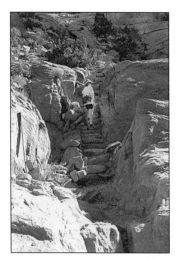

Photo 3

To Descend: Retrace your steps.

Calico Tank Peak

Hike: Calico Tank Peak — closed loop
Trailhead: Calico II pullout — marked
Distance: 3 miles — round trip
Elevation gain: 1,000 feet
Elevation peak: 5,200 feet
Time: 2 to 3 hours
Difficulty: 3
Danger level: 4
How easy to follow: 4
Children: no
Topo map: La Madre Mtn., NEV

Directions: The signed pullout for Calico Hills II Overlook is located 1.7 miles past the Scenic Loop gate.

Overview: The **route** goes down the trail, up the wash, and into a gully. About halfway up the gully, the route heads east into another gully, then through a tight passage and tunnel. The route passes Calico Tank before traveling to the peak.

Comments: This is one of the best short hikes in the book. The peak overlooks Calico Tank. After a rain, water in the tank can be five feet deep and 50 yards across.

The Hike: From the signed trailhead, the trail descends rapidly toward the wash. When the trail forks, take the first right,

Photo 1

then the first left. As the trail sinks into the wash, follow it; you'll pass three catch basins. At the top of the third catch basin, the path resumes. The path then begins to splinter, but the forks lead to a gully. Photo 1 is the gully seen from the trailhead. If the catch basins are filled with water, scramble up the sandstone to the west (left) of them. Continue toward the gully. Climb down the sandstone and onto any of the numerous paths below.

Once in the gully, stay near the west (left) wall and climb on the sandstone. About halfway up, another gully comes in from the east (right). A large pinion pine stands at the entrance. Scramble toward the pine as indicated in Photo 2.

Look for an obscure path that heads to the pine in Photo 2. The path avoids most of the scrub oak. Once past the pine, hike 40 yards along a sandstone ledge on the left wall of the gully, then drop down into the gully.

Photo 3 shows boulders blocking the gully and the ledge system you climb on to get around them. Zigzag back and forth on the ledges until you're past the boulders. In about 40 yards, another set of boulders blocks the gully. Small hikers can go under the boulder farthest on the left; the rest must climb over the boulders (class III). (See Photo 4.) Once past this second obstacle, it's a short jaunt up the gully, then up the sloping left wall to an area of level sandstone.

From the level sandstone, climb down 30 feet and drop into a slick rock passage. A small pinion pine sits above the passage. Head north (left) in the passage until it narrows. (See Photo 5.)

Remove your pack before entering the narrow part of the passage. As you're squeezing through the passage, look at Calico Tank Peak. (See Photo 6.) Stay in the passage until the walls withdraw. Go left (300 degrees) and hike about 30 yards along the base of the wall. Weave around the scrub oak and scramble up the wall. The pinnacle in Photo 7 serves as a landmark; the hiker shows where to scramble up the wall.

After climbing the wall (class II), you'll immediately step over a twisted log and hike 30 yards to a tunnel. (See Photo 8.) You can either go through the tunnel or climb over it. On the other side of the tunnel, a passage forms. Hike 15 yards up the passage and scramble into the less prominent right passage

(300 degrees). (See Photo 9.)

The passage heads NW, levels out for 30 yards, then narrows to an opening just wide enough to climb through (class III). Continue hiking near the right wall of the passage. When it splits, hike into the right fork. In about 50 yards you'll come to a high point where Calico Tank Peak comes into view. Photo 10 was taken from the high point.

Notice the varnish on the right side of Tank Peak; use it as a landmark for now. Your next destination is the white chipped sandstone circled in Photo 10. Al-

Photo 2

Photo 3

Photo 4

though there are many ways to go, I recommend traversing the left wall and heading NW (330 degrees) toward the pinion pine also circled in Photo 10.

From the pinion, hike to the white chipped sandstone and follow a faint path. Once the path ends, veer right and scramble up the red sandstone mound covered with yellow lichens. To your right lie the marble sandstone blocks circled in Photo 11. Scramble over to them.

Climb between the two huge pieces of

Photo 5

Photo 6

boulder that's been split in half, then turn left and climb the chute. Head NW (305 degrees) into a passage. (See Photo 12.) Veer to the right when the passage divides, climb an angled wall, and hike 40 yards to a vertical wall with black varnish.

At the wall, go left 30 yards to the point where the hiker in Photo 13 is climbing the angled wall. Once up, you'll see Calico Tank. Continue 30 yards in the same direction to a pile of boul-

Photo 7

Photo 8

Photo 9

ders. To your right is a steep beehive ramp that narrows into a chute near the top; scramble up it. (See Photo 14.) Once you're above the chute, you'll come to a semi-flat area. On the left are a couple of 30-foot sandstone mounds stacked on top of each other. Photo 15 shows a hiker at the base of the highest mound.

Scramble up to this point. (We built a pile of rocks to shorten the one long step needed to start the climb to the top of the sandstone mound.) Now head for the pinion pine at the top of the sandstone. Turn right just before the pinion and scramble up the sandstone. Go left 50 yards to the highest point. A small cairn marks the peak.

Calico Tank is to the south; use it as a landmark for your descent. Turtlehead and Turtlehead Jr. lie NW. If it's windy at the peak, there's a small natural shelter just below it.

To Descend: You have a number of options. You can scramble down to Calico Tank, follow the Calico Tank Trail to Sandstone Quarry, then take the Grand Circle Trail back to the trailhead (Calico II pull-out). Another option is to retrace your steps. The third and most popular option is to take a short-cut back to the trailhead.

If you choose option three, begin by retracing your steps. Scramble east toward the pinion. Descend the sandstone mound to Calico Tank. Scramble up the east wall of the tank and go left along

Tank Peak

Photo 10

Photo 11   **Photo 12**

the wall. Descend the same dry wash and veer left into the passage. Descend through the crack and go between the two boulder halves. From this point, angle toward the east end of the giant red and white sandstone wall, which lies to the SW. Find and follow a path that heads south along the wall. Eventually, you'll see the trailhead at Calico II parking lot. You're looking down the same gully you first hiked up, only you're farther up the gully. While descending the gully, you'll pass the pine that marks the entrance to the east gully you scrambled up earlier. You've made a loop; continue descending the same gully, staying near the right wall. The gully divides near the bottom (not obvious on the way up); go into the right fork.

Soon you'll come out onto one of the many paths that lead to and from the gully. Scrub oak is abundant in this area. Follow any of the paths to the catch basins. Once past the basins, you can see the trail leading to the parking lot.

Photo 13

Photo 14

Photo 15

◆ ◆ ◆

Britt's Loop

Hike: Britt's Loop — closed loop
Trailhead: Calico II pullout — marked
Distance: 2 miles — round trip
Elevation gain: 800 feet
Elevation peak: none
Time: 2 hours
Difficulty: 3
Danger level: 4
How easy to follow: 4
Children: no
Topo map: La Madre Mtn., NEV

Slot
+ tunnel

Directions: The signed pullout for Calico Hills II Overlook is located 1.7 miles past the Scenic Loop gate.

Overview: The **route** goes down the trail, across the wash, and into a gully. About halfway up the gully, the route heads east into another gully and through a passage, then loops back into the first gully.

Comments: This scrambling route has it all, including a passage so narrow that you'll have to exhale to fit through it and a tunnel to hike through. This is a loop hike, so you don't have to backtrack.

The Hike: From the signed trailhead, the trail descends rapidly toward the wash. When the trail forks, take the first right, then the first left. As the trail sinks into

Photo 1

Photo 2

the wash, follow it; you'll pass three catch basins. At the top of the third catch basin, the path resumes. The path then begins to splinter, but the forks lead to a gully. Photo 1 is the gully seen from the trailhead.

If the catch basins are filled with water, scramble up the sandstone to the west (left) of the catch basins. Continue toward the gully; climb down the sandstone and onto any of the numerous paths that lead to the gully.

Once in the gully, stay near the west (left) wall and climb on the sandstone. About halfway up, an obvious gully comes in from the east (right). A large pinion pine stands at the entrance. Scramble toward the pine as indicated in Photo 2.

Look for an obscure path that heads toward the pine. The path avoids most of the scrub oak. Hike 40 yards along a sandstone ledge on the left wall of the gully, then drop down into the east-heading gully.

Photo 3

Photo 3 shows boulders blocking the gully and the ledge system you climb on to get around them. Zigzag back and forth on the ledges until you're past the boulders. In 40 yards, more boulders block the

Photo 4

Photo 5

gully. Small hikers can go under the boulder farthest on the left; the rest have to climb over the boulders (class III). (See Photo 4.) Once past this second obstacle, it's a short jaunt up the gully, then up the sloping left wall to an area of level sandstone.

From the level sandstone, climb down 30 feet and drop into a slick rock passage. A small pinion pine sits above the passage. Head north (left) in the passage until it narrows. (See Photo 5.)

Remove your pack before traversing the narrow part of the passage. Stay in the passage until the walls withdraw. Go left (300 degrees) and hike 30 yards along the base of the wall. Weave around the scrub oak and scramble up the wall. The pinnacle in Photo 6 serves as a landmark; the hiker shows where to scramble up the wall.

After climbing the wall (class II), you'll immediately step over a log and head for the tunnel in Photo 7. You can go through the tunnel or climb over it. On the other side, a passage forms. Hike 15 yards in the passage and scramble into the less-prominent right passage (300 degrees). (See Photo 8.)

Pinnacle

Photo 6

The passage heads NW, levels out for 30 yards, and then narrows to an opening just wide enough to climb through (class III). Continue north (340 degrees) for 40 to 50 yards until the sandstone tower with black varnish comes into view. (See Photo 9.)

The scrub oak about halfway up the tower should help you identify it. Head west (left) toward the tower. You'll scramble down the sandstone to a flat area where a path forms. Follow it up a small rise to a pinion pine. From this vantage point, you'll see the trailhead at the Calico II parking lot. You're looking down the same gully you first hiked up, only you're farther up the gully. Descend the gully. You'll pass the pine that marks the entrance to the east gully that you scrambled up earlier. At this point you've made a loop; continue de-

Photo 7

scending the same gully and stay near the right wall. The gully divides near the bottom (not obvious on the way up); go into the right fork. Soon you'll come out onto one of the many paths that lead to and from the gully. Scrub oak is abundant in this area. Follow any of the paths to the catch basins. Once past the basins, you can see the trail leading to the parking lot.

Photo 8

Photo 9

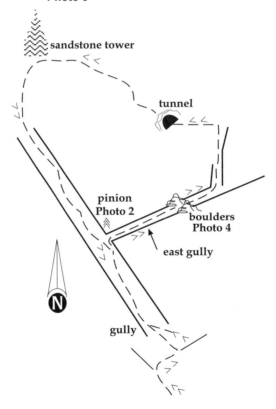

Sandstone Quarry Loop

Hike: Sandstone Quarry Loop — closed loop
Trailhead: Sandstone Quarry — marked
Distance: 2.5 miles — round trip
Elevation gain: less than 200 feet
Elevation peak: none
Time: 1 to 2 hours
Difficulty: 1
Danger level: 1
How easy to follow: 2
Children: yes
Topo map: La Madre Mtn., NEV

Directions: The signed parking lot for Sandstone Quarry is located 2.8 miles past the Scenic Loop gate.

Overview: The **trail** heads NW before turning into a **path.** It drops into a wash and loops back onto the trail.

Comments: The partial-loop hike takes you through desert terrain, past sandstone crags, and near the base of Turtlehead Peak.

The Hike: Hike NW 75 yards along the gravel trail until it disappears into a shallow wash. Walk NW 10 yards in the wash to a point where the trail resumes. (You'll see large sandstone rocks that resemble overgrown children's blocks; stay to the left of them.) Continue on the trail to a major fork, where a small sign indicates to take the left fork to Turtlehead Peak. About 100 yards after the fork, you'll climb a small hill. When the trail forks again, take the right fork and hike down the hill and into the wash. Walk about 50 yards NW in the wash until the trail resumes on the right side of the wash. The trail then forks again; take the right fork and follow it up another small hill. The trail empties into the wash again. Follow any of the paths through the wash; they all travel in the same direction. Continue NW in the wash until the trail climbs another hill. (See Photo 1.)

Photo 1

The trail veers to the right (30 degrees), goes between two sandstone crags, and then heads directly for Turtlehead Peak. In the distance, you'll see the path climb a hill; however, you don't want to follow the path. At the fork just before the hill, take the right (less prominent) fork and follow it to a major wash. Go south (right) in the wash and walk toward the sandstone wall ahead. When you're within 30 yards of the wall, look for a path that comes in from the right. Go west (right) onto the path; it parallels the wall. In 100 yards, go south (left) onto a more defined path that heads toward the parking lot. You'll hike between two sandstone crags.

About 30 yards after the sandstone crags, a faint path comes in from the right. (If you go across a white sandstone slab, you've gone too far.) Go right (250 degrees) onto the faint path; it soon becomes more defined and weaves between two sandstone crags before emptying onto a gently sloping sandstone slab. As you hike down the slab, the *trail* you started out on lies about 75 yards ahead. The *path* resumes at the center of the far edge of the slab. The path veers left, climbs a hill, and connects with the trail. Go SE (left) onto the trail. From this spot you can see the parking lot. Follow the trail as it empties into the wash. From here, you can follow the wash or the trail back to the parking lot. The wash is more direct. Most of the time you can see either the parking lot or the Scenic Loop Road, and your direction of travel is obvious.

♦ ♦ ♦

Sandstone Quarry Overlook

Hike: Sandstone Quarry Overlook — up and back
Trailhead: Sandstone Quarry — marked
Distance: 1 mile — round trip
Elevation gain: 365 feet
Elevation peak: 4,708 feet
Time: 1 hour
Difficulty: 2
Danger level: 4
How easy to follow: 4
Children: no
Topo map: La Madre Mtn., NEV

Directions: The signed parking lot for Sandstone Quarry is located 2.8 miles past the Scenic Loop gate.

Overview: The hike follows part of the Grand Circle **Trail,** then takes a cutoff **path** to the wash. Once across the wash, you'll hike a **route** up the sandstone to an overlook.

Overlook

Photo 1

Comments: A quick scrambling route with lots of class III climbing. Photo 1 shows the overlook.

The Hike: The hike starts where the Grand Circle Trail intersects the NE corner of the Sandstone

Photo 2   **Photo 3**

Quarry parking lot. A small trail sign marks the intersection. Follow the Grand Circle Trail as it heads east, paralleling the gravel entrance road to Sandstone Quarry parking lot. After 100 yards the trail climbs a small hill and then descends slightly as it heads east toward the Calico II pullout. The boulder circled in Photo 2 serves as a landmark. Once you are directly across from the boulder, take any path that leads to the wash below. Cross the wash and scramble up the sandstone mound. (See Photo 3.)

Veer left and climb the second mound to the scrub oak circled in Photo 4. Go between the left wall and scrub oak and head west (290 degrees) up the red sandstone as shown in Photo 5. As you head west, the sandstone changes from red to white. Walls on both sides narrow, making it easy to stay in this progressively steeper passage. Scramble up the steep ramp to the four-foot-wide passage. Once through, the terrain levels out and

Photo 4

Passage ↓

Photo 5

La Madre Mountain comes into view.

To your left stands a 15-foot-high sandstone wall. Scramble to the top of the wall by going east around the front of it, through the scrub oak, and over the boulders. At the top, another wall stands about 30 feet to the south. The overlook is at the top of this wall; however, you must go around to the south side. Descend to the west (right) about 30 feet to a chute on the left. (See Photo 6.) Climb the chute, turn left, and scramble up to the overlook; it's a group of flat sandstone mounds. If you're at the correct overlook, you'll see a three-foot-high scrub oak in the center. To the east lie Calico Hills I and II, to the west sits Sandstone Quarry, and to the NW looms the gray peak of Turtlehead.

To Descend: Retrace your steps. Climb down the chute, descend to the bottom of the second wall, and turn right into the four-foot-wide passage. Descend the passage and head east toward the red sandstone. Walk toward the spiral-looking sandstone pinnacle, turn right, and scramble down the sandstone toward the wash. From there, follow any path that leads to Grand Circle Trail. Turn right onto the trail and follow it back to Sandstone Quarry parking lot.

Photo 6

◆ ◆ ◆

Mescalito

Hike: Mescalito — up and back
Trailhead: Pine Creek — marked
Distance: 8 miles — round trip
Elevation gain: 1,440 feet
Elevation peak: 5,440 feet
Time: 6 to 7 hours
Difficulty: 4
Danger level: 5
How easy to follow: 5
Children: no
Topo map: Blue Diamond, NEV and Mountain Springs, NEV

Directions: The signed parking area for Pine Creek Canyon is 10.3 miles past the Scenic Loop gate.

Overview: The hike follows Pine Creek **Trail** into the south fork of Pine Creek. The **route** goes through the north fork, then climbs a false peak before going to the real peak.

Comments: Only people who are in good shape, are comfortable on class III rock, and have a good sense of direction should attempt this hike. Look for numerous cairns along the route. At the peak, you'll look almost straight down into the south fork of Pine Creek. This is the only known non-technical route to Mescalito. (See Photo 1.)

The Hike: Pine Creek Trail descends to the south before turning west toward the mouth of the canyon. When you see the concrete foundation of the old Wilson homestead, you've hiked

Photo 1

four-fifths of a mile. As you approach the mouth of Pine Creek, the Mescalito, a pyramid-shaped peak, splits the canyon into north and south forks. The trail veers north as it parallels the stream that flows from the canyon. The trail soon crosses a dry wash and leads you to the south bank. You can enter the wash at this point, but farther on it's filled with water. You don't want to get wet if the water is cold, especially if you're hiking in the shade. Don't expect the water temperature to be bearable unless the weather has been hot.

The trail heads south and crosses another dry wash. This marks your departure from the established trail, which turns east—away from the canyon. Follow the path at the bottom of the wash and go toward the canyon. When the path forks in 20 yards, take the right fork. The path goes between two large boulders and over a rock-filled area before it becomes easier to follow. It then weaves through manzanita and scrub oak before crossing the wash again. The path has a slight incline as it heads NW; you should pass a burnt tree.

The paths spider-web in so many directions that it's almost impossible to follow the same route each time. At this point

you're so close to the entrance of the canyon that you should select the path of least resistance. No matter which way you choose, you'll soon be above the wash, with a number of paths leading down

Photo 2

into it. Pick a path that's relatively free of brush.

Once in the wash, boulder through the south fork of Pine Creek until the canyon divides. You'll see three ponderosa pines (one dead) standing guard just before the divide. To the right of the dead pine is a large red boulder. Go between the dead tree and the boulder into the north fork; I call it the Mescalito Fork. In 50 yards hike around the left side of a 20-foot-high red boulder. Traverse the boulder field that lies on the left bank of the Mescalito Fork. Continue for 100 yards before

Photo 3

dropping back into the wash. When you come to three huge gray boulders, go around them to the right. About 100 yards past the gray boulders, brush divides the wash into left and right forks; hike into the left one. When brush divides the wash again, take the left fork. Continue up the canyon until you see the boulder slide pictured in Photo 2. It will be to your right.

About 50 yards *before* the boulder slide, the south (left) wall of the canyon recesses about one-third of the way up the wall. You'll see trees and vegetation growing in the recess. Use this for a landmark to locate the boulder slide both now and when you descend.

Scramble NW (300 degrees) up the boulder slide for 50 yards. Just past the first pinion pine, a faint path starts to your left. Follow it (you'll hike past two more

Photo 4

Photo 5

pinions) until you reach a sandstone wall marked by erosion holes. Climb the wall to the steep slanted ramp that leads to the alcove, but don't scramble all the way to it. (See Photo 3.) Instead, 30 yards before the alcove, head east (right) and go between the large boulder and scrub oak. Look for a large cairn. To avoid the brush in front of you, descend 50 yards to a sandstone ledge that overlooks the canyon. Head NE along the precarious ledge (it becomes wider) for 100 yards until you reach the side of a large horseshoe-shaped wash. You must get above and past the wash. Head NE up the wash as shown in Photo 4. The large sandstone boulder circled in the photo is your landmark.

Once up, head NE toward a tree that looks like a windsock. (See Photo 5.) Just below the tree is a chute that leads up to the ridgeline. You must climb to the ridgeline before you can get to Mescalito Peak. There's a huge gorge that you can't see from this point; the only way to circumvent the gorge is to get above it.

Photo 6

As you approach the tree, you'll see that it's at the top of a wall. Parallel the wall and scramble up the chute (Photo 6). If you hike onto red sandstone, you've gone too far. At the top of the chute you have a fantastic view of Bridge Mountain and the north fork of Pine Creek. From here you'll head east along the top of the

Photo 7

Photo 8

ridgeline, then descend about 300 feet to a saddle before Mescalito Peak.

As you hike east, the red-colored Mescalito Peak comes into view. Continue east 40 yards to a point where you have to descend. Scramble down to the red sandstone on the right, then veer left and head straight for Mescalito Peak. You'll hike across more red sandstone. When you cliff-out on a flat mound of white sandstone, scramble down along the base of a wall on your right. Hike NE and go left of the dead tree and the boulder in Photo 7.

Just beyond the dead tree, wedge through two boulders and continue 40 yards to the pinion that marks the top of a chute. (See Photo 8.) In 40 yards the chute becomes brushy. To avoid the brush, traverse 10 yards along a

Photo 9

Photo 10   **Photo 11**

narrow sandstone ledge to your right. Descend 15 yards (class III) on the beehive crag and scramble off the right side of the crag. Follow a path through brush (about 30 yards) onto sandstone. Continue around the boulder seen in Photo 9. From here, you'll see the saddle. It's only 40 feet below—you're almost down!

Stay close to the boulder as you make your way to a dirt-filled chute that leads down to the next level. Now, hug the wall as you hike past a pinion and scrub oak. To the SE (right) is the final sandstone crag you must climb down to get to the saddle. Once you're on the final mound, look SE to see your next destination. (See Photo 10.) Climb off the south (right) side of the mound to the saddle (class III).

Photo 12

Once at the saddle, follow the obvious path across the saddle to the sandstone. Walk about 20 yards along the ledge until you come to the top of a deep chute. A gutter provides a class III crawl past the chute. Once you're on the flat sandstone mound in Photo 10, look for the passage; it will be on your left, just past the boulders. (See Photo 11.) Go through the passage and climb down. You're now at the top of the gorge you had to go around. (Photo 12 shows hikers scrambling around the gorge.)

Once on the other side, continue east for 75 yards. Before the sandstone turns from white to red, veer left and follow a faint path through the vegetation toward the two red sandstone crags. (See Photo 13.) About halfway to the sandstone crags, go right and scramble up

Photo 13

the steep red ramp toward the first pinion in Photo 14. Turn right (NE), go under the second pinion, and walk 50 yards along the wide ledge toward the highest sandstone crag. (See Photo 15.) There's a huge drop-off on your right side.

Veer left between the crags at the huge cairn. Continue another 50 yards and look to your right for the cairn that sits at the peak. You made it! Few people have hiked to this peak. The view down into the south fork of Pine Creek is awesome! To the north are Bridge Mountain and Bridge Point; to the south stand Juniper Peak and Rainbow Wall and Peak. Pine Creek Trail snakes through the desert out to the east.

To Descend: Retrace your steps.

Photo 14

Photo 15

♦ ♦ ♦

Gunsight Notch Peak

Hike: Gunsight Notch Peak — up and back
Trailhead: Pine Creek — marked
Distance: 6.5 miles — round trip
Elevation gain: 2,200 feet
Elevation peak: 6,200 feet
Time: 4 to 5 hours
Difficulty: 5
Danger level: 3
How easy to follow: 4
Children: no
Topo map: Blue Diamond, NEV and Mountain Springs, NEV

Directions: The signed parking area for Pine Creek Canyon is 10.3 miles past the Scenic Loop gate.

Overview: Follow Pine Creek **Trail** into the canyon. From here it's a bouldering **route** through the canyon; you'll go left at the first and second forks. Go left into Gunsight Notch Canyon and scramble to the notch and peak.

Comments: If the view from the notch doesn't take your breath away, you're clinically dead. This is a must-do hike. Just before the peak, you come to the top of Gunsight Notch. This narrow, three-foot-wide notch looks down almost a thousand feet into Juniper Canyon. To the right of the notch stands the 1,200-foot vertical Rainbow Wall.

The Hike: Pine Creek Trail descends south, then turns west toward the mouth of the canyon. You'll pass the turnoff for

Photo 1

the Fire Ecology Trail; it loops back into this trail 30 yards ahead. When the trail passes the concrete foundation of the old Wilson homestead, you've hiked four-fifths of a mile. As you approach the mouth of Pine Creek, the Mescalito, a pyramid-shaped peak, splits the canyon into north and south forks. The trail veers north as it parallels the stream that flows from the canyon. The trail soon crosses a dry wash and leads you to the south bank. You can enter the wash at this point, but farther on it's filled with water. You don't want to get wet if the water is cold, especially if you're hiking in the shade. Don't expect the water temperature to be bearable unless the weather has been hot.

The trail heads south and crosses another dry wash. This marks your departure from the established trail, which turns east—away from the canyon. Follow the path at the bottom of the wash as it heads toward the canyon. When the path forks in 20 yards, take the right fork. The path goes between two large boulders and over a rock-filled area before it becomes easier to follow. It then weaves through manzanita and scrub oak before crossing the wash again. The path has a slight incline as it heads NW; you should pass a burnt tree.

The paths spider-web in so many directions that it's almost impossible to follow the same route each time. At this point

Photo 2

you're so close to the entrance of the canyon that you should select the path of least resistance. No matter which way you choose, you'll soon be above the wash, with a number of paths leading down into it. Pick a path that's relatively free of brush.

Once in the wash, boulder through the south fork of Pine Creek until the canyon divides. You'll see three ponderosa pines (one dead) standing guard just before the divide. Hike into the south (left) fork of the canyon, just to the left of the third (largest) pine, and

Photo 3

scramble up the pinkish boulders. This fork (the south-south fork of Pine Creek) has plenty of class II and class III bouldering.

Once you're in the fork, you'll scramble up a candy-striped ramp of sandstone. You'll be heading due south. In 100 yards a five-foot boulder blocks your way; go around it to the right. As you continue bouldering your way through the canyon, it looks like the canyon ends. But it makes a sharp left, which isn't apparent until you come to that spot. At the sharp left, stay near the right wall to avoid the brush. Once the canyon turns left, you'll be heading south again. When the canyon curves to the right, stay near the right side of the wash to avoid the brush.

Soon the canyon divides again. You'll hike into the south (left) fork at the divide. There's a trick to hiking into this fork. Walk

Photo 4

past the first wash that goes up the south fork of the canyon and hike into the second wash. It's free of brush. A good landmark to watch for is the overhang off the left wall of the canyon's entrance. The second wash lies just beyond the overhang. You'll go SE up the wash; it's narrow at first. You're now in the south-south-south fork of Pine Creek.

You'll come to a spot where a huge boulder is wedged into the right wall of the wash. Scramble between the boulder and the right wall (class III). Once past the boulder, stay near the right wall of the canyon. Although it's obvious that the canyon divides up ahead, it's easy to miss the wash that leads into Gunsight Notch Canyon. (See Photo 1.)

Gunsight Notch Canyon veers left; the canyon to the right is Terrace Canyon. Photo 2 shows the start of the wash that leads up the canyon. Use the overhang rock in Photo 2 as a landmark. Photo 3 is an overview of the route up the canyon. (You can't see the peak or notch until you have climbed out of the canyon.)

You'll boulder 100 yards up the wash before you enter the red sandstone floor of the canyon. This is the prettiest canyon in Red Rock. Keep scrambling SE up the steep canyon floor. The right wall becomes sheer. It's a strenuous scramble to the top of the canyon. Near the head of the canyon, there are a lot of class III sections. You can avoid them by veering left and paralleling the canyon. Soon, the peak comes into view on the left. (See Photo 4.) The notch, to the right of the peak, looks like a saddle from below. Scramble to the notch and peer down. That's Juniper Canyon, almost 1,000 feet below. To your right stands the 1,200-foot Rainbow Wall. This is an incredible view!

From the notch hike NE 120 yards along the east (Juniper Canyon) side to the peak. You're treated to additional vistas along this route. Aim for the dead tree that sits at the peak. Allow time to enjoy the view. Check out Rainbow Wall; you might see climbers. Rainbow Wall is normally a two-day climb, meaning that climbers spend the night on the wall. Be sure to sign the register. (Special thanks to Neil Sobelson, who told me about this awesome hike.)

To Descend: Retrace your steps down through Gunsight Notch Canyon and back out through Pine Creek to the trail.

◆ ◆ ◆

Terrace Canyon

Hike: Terrace Canyon — up and back
Trailhead: Pine Creek — marked
Distance: 5 miles — round trip
Elevation gain: 1,084 feet
Elevation peak: none
Time: 3 to 4 hours
Difficulty: 3
Danger level: 3
How easy to follow: 3
Children: no
Topo map: Blue Diamond, NEV and Mountain
Springs, NEV

Directions: The signed parking area for Pine Creek Canyon is
10.3 miles past the Scenic Loop gate.

Overview: Follow Pine Creek **Trail** into the canyon. From here
it's a bouldering **route** through the canyon, going left at both
the first and second forks to Terrace Canyon.

Comments: This is one of the best bouldering routes in Red
Rock. Terrace Canyon gets its name from the cascading dry
falls that resemble a rolling terrace.

The Hike: Pine Creek Trail descends south, then turns west toward the mouth of the canyon. When the trail passes the concrete foundation of the old Wilson homestead, you've hiked
four-fifths of a mile. As you approach the mouth of Pine Creek,
the Mescalito, a pyramid-shaped peak, splits the canyon into
north and south forks. The trail veers north as it parallels the

Photo 1

stream that flows from the canyon. The trail soon crosses a dry wash and leads you to the south bank. You can enter the wash at this point, but farther on it's filled with water. You don't want to get wet if the water is cold, especially if you're hiking in the shade. Don't expect the water temperature to be bearable unless the weather is hot.

The trail heads south and crosses another dry wash. This marks your departure from the established trail, which turns east—away from the canyon. Follow the path at the bottom of the wash as it heads toward the canyon. When the path forks in 20 yards, take the right fork. The path goes between two large boulders and over a rock-filled area before it becomes easier to follow. It then weaves through manzanita and scrub oak before crossing the wash again. The path has a slight incline as it heads NW; you should pass a burnt tree.

The paths spider-web in so many directions that it's almost impossible to follow the same route each time. At this point you're so close to the entrance of the canyon that you should select the path of least resistance. No matter which way you choose, you'll soon be above the wash, with a number of paths leading down into it. Pick one that's relatively free of brush.

Once in the wash, boulder through the south fork of Pine Creek until the canyon divides. You'll see three ponderosa pines (one dead) standing guard just before the divide. Hike into the south (left) fork of the canyon just to the left of the third (largest) pine and scramble up the pinkish boulders. This fork (the south-south fork of Pine Creek) offers plenty of class II and class III bouldering. No ropes needed

Once you're in the fork, you'll scramble up a candy-striped ramp of sandstone. At this point you'll be heading due south. In 100 yards a five-foot boulder blocks your way; go around it to the right. As you continue bouldering your way through the canyon, it looks like the canyon ends. But it makes a sharp left, which isn't apparent until you come to that spot. At the sharp left, stay near the right wall to avoid the brush. Once the canyon turns to the left, you'll be heading south again. When

Photo 2

the canyon curves right, stay near the right side of the wash to avoid the brush.

Soon the canyon divides again. You'll hike into the south (left) fork at the divide. There's a trick to hiking into this fork. Walk past the first wash that goes up the south fork of the canyon and hike into the second wash, which is free of brush. A good landmark to watch for is the overhang off the left wall of the canyon's entrance. The second wash lies just beyond the overhang. You'll head SE up the wash, which is narrow at first. You will now be in the south-south-south fork of Pine Creek.

You'll come to a spot where a huge boulder is wedged into the right wall of the wash. Scramble between the boulder and the right wall (class III). Once past the boulder, stay near the right wall of the canyon. Again, the canyon divides; hike into the *right* fork. At the start of the right fork, the wash divides; hike in the section on the right to avoid the brush. There's some brush in this right fork, but not too much. You'll soon go under an overhang on the right wall of the canyon. Just beyond the overhang, follow a path that goes around a blockage to the right. You're now at the start of Terrace Canyon. (Photo 1 was taken on January 1, 1998. That's ice in the picture!) Continue south up a series of cascading dry falls to the large fallen tree in Photo 2. This is the perfect place to have lunch and relax before returning to the trailhead.

To Descend: Retrace your steps.

♦ ♦ ♦

Ice Box Canyon Loop

Hike: Ice Box Canyon Loop — closed loop
Trailhead: Ice Box Canyon overflow parking — not marked
Distance: 2.5 miles — round trip
Elevation gain: less than 100 feet
Elevation peak: none
Time: 1 to 2 hours
Difficulty: 1
Danger level: 1
How easy to follow: 1
Children: yes
Topo map: La Madre Mtn., NEV

Directions: The signed turnoff for Ice Box Canyon is located 8 miles past the Scenic Loop gate. The trailhead begins at the overflow parking area on the left side of the road.

Overview: The **trail** passes near Willow Springs, Lost Creek, and Ice Box Canyon.

Comments: This is a perfect hike for families or for beginners; it's an especially pleasant hike when the cactus and flowers are in bloom in April and May. Since this is a loop, you can also begin the hike at Lost Creek trailhead and hike clockwise.

The Hike: The trail heads NE and climbs a steep hill. At the top of the hill, it connects with the unmarked Grand Circle Trail (GCT). Go west (left) onto the GCT and follow it as it crosses the Scenic Loop road and continues toward White Rock Hills Peak. Turn SW (left) on the unmarked White Rock/Willow Springs/La Madre Trail when you intersect it. Soon you'll see the parking lot for Lost Creek/Children's Discovery Trail. When you're 50 yards from the parking lot, go left onto any path and cross the road to the signed Lost Creek/Children's Discovery parking lot.

Hike the Lost Creek Trail; don't go on the Children's Discovery Trail. In 75 yards go left onto the signed SMYC Trail. This is a new trail 1.1 miles long that connects with the Ice Box Canyon Trail. (If you want to make a side trip to Lost Creek Waterfall, stay on Lost Creek Trail instead of going left onto SMYC Trail. When you return on Lost Creek Trail, go SE (right) onto SMYC Trail. This adds a half-mile to the hike.)

The SMYC Trail heads SE, crosses two washes, then goes along the base of some sandstone crags. When the trail turns east, you'll see the parking lot for Ice Box Canyon in the distance. The trail descends across a drainage area, then climbs to a high point where you can see Ice Box Canyon Trail. When you intersect Ice Box Canyon Trail, go left and follow it back to the parking lot.

◆ ◆ ◆

Dale's Trail

Hike: Dale's Trail — up and back
Trailhead: Ice Box Canyon — marked
Distance: 4.5 miles — round trip
Elevation gain: –200 feet (descent) starting from Ice
Box Canyon
Elevation peak: none
Time: 2 to 3 hours
Difficulty: 1
Danger level: 1
How easy to follow: 1
Children: yes
Topo map: La Madre Mtn., NEV

Directions: The signed turnoff for Ice Box Canyon is located
8 miles past the Scenic Loop gate. The pulloff is on the right
side of the road, with overflow parking on the left side.

Overview: The **trail** heads south across the desert, where it
intersects with Pine Creek Trail.

Comments: This BLM trail, constructed in 1998, connects Ice
Box Canyon Trail with Pine Creek Trail. It's easier to start from
Ice Box Canyon than from Pine Creek, because there's an overall loss in elevation. If you start from Ice Box Canyon, you'll
have to hike back on this trail. If you start from Pine Creek, I
suggest you and your hiking partner leave one car at Ice Box
Canyon and drive a second car to Pine Creek.

The Hike: Ice Box Canyon Trail heads SSW and crosses Red
Rock Wash. About 75 yards past the wash, turn east (left) on

the signed Dale's Trail. The trail starts off easy as it heads toward Pine Creek. You'll soon cross the first of many washes. On the other side of the first wash, look north (left) for a good view of Turtlehead Peak and Calico Hills. If it's late in the afternoon, the Calico Hills look as though they're on fire.

The trail stays about 100 yards away from the base of the sandstone mountains. As the trail turns south, you'll travel near the base of Bridge Point. From this angle you can see that it's impossible to climb Bridge Point without ropes. In a short amount of time, the Pine Creek parking lot comes into view. You'll cross two more washes and descend a slope before coming to a sign that marks "Skull Rock," a large red boulder that looks like a skull. In less than 100 yards, you'll intersect Pine Creek Trail. If you want to go to the Pine Creek parking lot, take a left; go right if you want to hike into Pine Creek Canyon or to turn around and head back to Ice Box Canyon.

♦ ♦ ♦

Arnight Trail

Hike: Arnight Trail — up and back
Trailhead: Oak Creek Canyon Parking Lot — marked
Distance: 3.2 miles — round trip
Elevation gain: less than 200 feet
Elevation peak: none
Time: 1 to 2 hours
Difficulty: 1
Danger level: 1
How easy to follow: 1
Children: yes
Topo map: Blue Diamond, NEV

Directions: The signed turnoff road for Oak Creek Canyon is located 12 miles past the Scenic Loop gate. Turn right on the gravel road and drive three-quarters of a mile to the trailhead.

Overview: The BLM **trail** heads west toward Pine Creek.

Comments: Arnight serves as a connector trail between Oak Creek parking lot and Pine Creek Canyon. Arnight Trail intersects Pine Creek Trail a little past the old Wilson homestead.

The Hike: The signed trail starts in the NW corner of the parking lot and follows an abandoned road. In less than 200 yards, the trail makes a hard right. As the trail heads west toward Bridge Mountain, it becomes sandy in a few areas. To the left is the multicolored Rainbow Peak. Large scrub oak bushes grow next to the trail as it crosses a wide wash. The trail temporarily heads for Juniper Canyon, then passes it. Off in the distance to your right is the parking lot for Pine Creek. You'll cross a deep wash before coming to an intersection. If you want to go into Juniper Canyon, turn left; otherwise, make a right and continue on the Arnight Trail.

About 40 yards after the intersection, a path forks off to the right, but stay on the Arnight Trail. It heads west around a slope that overlooks Pine Creek Trail. You'll descend the slope and connect with a fork of the Pine Creek Trail. At this point you can either turn around and return to Oak Creek Canyon or go onto the Pine Creek Trail.

If you want to hike the Pine Creek Trail, go right at the intersection. You'll soon cross a branch of Pine Creek. About 200 yards past the creek, you'll come to what's left of the old Wilson homestead. The main Pine Creek Trail lies NW 50 feet from the foundation. Once on the main Pine Creek Trail, go right to the Pine Creek trailhead or left into Pine Creek.

Tired of driving the Scenic Loop? Here's a way to avoid the 13-mile drive and add an additional 3 miles to this short hike. Park at the Scenic Loop exit along State Route 159 (2 miles past the entrance to Red Rock). Walk along the Scenic Loop road a little less than a mile to the signed gravel road that goes to Oak Creek Canyon parking lot. Follow the gravel road to the trailhead. If you don't like walking on paved roads, watch for a path just a few yards south of the Scenic Loop road. Hike the path instead of walking on the pavement.

◆ MT. CHARLESTON AREA ◆

Mt. Charleston is part of the Spring Mountains, the mightiest mountain range in Southern Nevada. The range gets its name from the numerous springs hidden deep inside the mountains; it borders Las Vegas Valley on the west side and extends for 50 miles. No other major city and mountain range within such close proximity have such a difference in elevation. When you stand on Charleston Peak, you'll look down almost 10,000 feet to Las Vegas, yet you're only 30 miles from the Strip. Charleston Peak is named after Charleston, South Carolina.

The Mt. Charleston Area is home to the bristlecone pine tree, the oldest living thing on earth. (You'll walk past a 3,000-year-old bristlecone on the Mummy's Toe hike.) The area is also home to at least 30 endemic species. This is a rugged mountain range with many cliffs and deep canyons that hide natural treasures from the average hiker. You can discover these treasures if you accept the challenge of the more difficult routes.

Nothing compares to the exhilaration you'll feel when you stand on a peak few have stood on before. Six of the hikes in this section lead you to various exclusive peaks. The other six hikes are designed for families and weekend hikers. Whatever type of hiking experience you want, the hikes in the Mt. Charleston Area will satisfy it. For the latest updates and trail conditions, visit my Web site at: www.hikinglasvegas.com.

Directions to Mt. Charleston
For trailheads in the Kyle Canyon area of Mt. Charleston: From the Mirage on Las Vegas Boulevard (the Strip), go north 1.5 miles and turn west (left) onto Sahara. In less than 1 mile,

turn north (right) onto I-15. Take I-15 2 miles to U.S. 95 north. Take U.S. 95 north 14 miles to State Route 157.

For trailheads in Lee Canyon: From the Mirage on Las Vegas Boulevard (the Strip), go north 1.5 miles and turn west (left) onto Sahara. In less than 1 mile, turn north (right) onto I-15. Take I-15 2 miles to U.S. 95 north. Take U.S. 95 north 27 miles to State Route 156. See map on next page.

FAST FACTS—MT. CHARLESTON

Location: 35 miles NW of Las Vegas.

Directions: Drive north on U.S. 95, then turn west (left) on State Route 157 or State Route 156.

Visitor Center: Open only on weekends during the summer from 9 a.m. to 4 p.m., (702) 872-5486. Drive 18.4 miles along State Route 157. The Visitor Center is located by the Ranger Station on the left side of State Route 157.

Fee: $5 per car for parking at Cathedral Rock and Old Mills Campground.

Permits: None needed for day hiking.

Camping: Kyle Canyon, Fletcher View, Kyle Canyon RV Site, Hilltop, Mahogany Grove, McWilliams, and Dolemite. For reservations call (800) 280-CAMP (2267).

Elevation range: 7,000 feet to 11,918 feet.

Size: 316,000 acres.

Hikes: From 1 mile to 20 miles. All ranges of difficulty.

Dogs: Must be on a leash.

Horses: Designated trails.

Bikes: Yes, but the roads are narrow.

Mountain bikes: Designated trails.

Firearms: Not permitted.

Gasoline: None available.

Food and Lodging: Mt. Charleston Lodge, (702) 872-5408, and Mt. Charleston Hotel, (702) 872-5500.

Managed by: U.S. Forestry Service, (702) 873-8800.

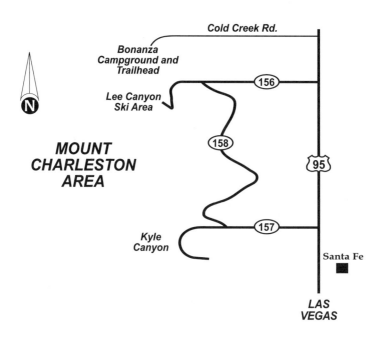

Difficulty Index: Mt. Charleston — 12 hikes

Easy	Moderate	Advanced
Desert Overlook: p. 162 Echo Loop: p. 148 Highway 158: p. 157 Little Falls: p. 146	Echo Overlook: p. 150 Ridge Route: p. 159	McFarland Peak: p. 189 Mummy's Chin: p. 176 Mummy's Forehead: p. 182 Mummy's Nose: p. 171 Mummy's Toe: p. 152 The Sisters: p. 164

◆ ◆ ◆

Little Falls

Hike: Little Falls — up and back
Trailhead: Cathedral Rock Temporary Trail/Echo
Trail — marked
Distance: 1 mile — round trip
Elevation gain: less than 200 feet
Elevation peak: none
Time: 30 to 45 minutes
Difficulty: 1
Danger level: 1
How easy to follow: 1
Children: yes
Topo map: Charleston Peak, NEV

Directions: Take U.S. 95 to State Route 157. Go left on 157 and drive 20.6 miles, then turn right onto Echo Drive at the hairpin curve. Drive 200 yards and turn left into a gravel parking area.

Overview: Head west, then SE on Echo **Trail,** then go west again for the last quarter-mile to Little Falls.

Comments: This is a perfect hike for beginners or for families. Early spring is the best time to see water flowing from the falls. You'll hike Echo Trail, also known as Cathedral Rock Temporary Trail, to Little Falls. Officially, there's not a Little Falls Trail, but that's what the locals call this part of Echo Trail.

The Hike: The hike starts at the Echo Trail sign. (See Photo 1 in the Echo Overlook hike, p. 151.) The trail weaves through aspens as it heads due west toward a wash. Once you're across the wash, a trail sign indicates the distance to Little Falls: a half-mile. The trail turns SE as it climbs a hill. An unmarked gravel road comes in from the left as an Echo Trail sign directs you to go right. In 200 yards, the trail forks. Go left and continue on Echo Trail. The trail levels out, and it's very scenic here as you pass through a thick grove of ponderosa pines and white firs. The trail crosses a wash before coming to a junction and another trail sign. Go west (right) as indicated by the trail sign.

The last quarter-mile to Little Falls starts off with a slight incline as the trail parallels a wash. When the trail goes through a wide gravel area, look for the continuation of the trail ahead, slightly to the left. The trail ends at Little Falls. Go ahead and explore the side paths that follow along the base of the walls that make up Little Falls.

To Descend: Retrace your steps. Go left at the first trail sign you see on the return trip.

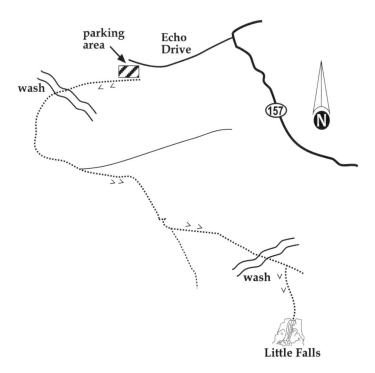

♦ ♦ ♦

Echo Loop

Hike: Echo Loop — closed loop
Trailhead: Cathedral Rock Temporary Trail/Echo Trail — marked
Distance: 1 mile — round trip
Elevation gain: less than 100 feet
Elevation peak: none
Time: 30 minutes
Difficulty: 1
Danger level: 1
How easy to follow: 2
Children: yes
Topo map: Charleston Peak, NEV

Directions: Take U.S. 95 to State Route 157. Go left on 157 and drive 20.6 miles. Turn right onto Echo Drive at the hairpin curve. Drive 200 yards and turn left into a gravel parking area.

Overview: The **trail** makes a large circle and passes near Little Falls and Cathedral Rock picnic area.

Comments: This is an easy loop hike for beginners.

The Hike: The hike starts at the Echo Trail sign. (See Photo 1 in the Echo Overlook hike, p. 151.) The trail weaves through aspens and heads due west toward a wash. Once you're across the wash, a trail sign indicates distances to various locations. The trail turns SE as it climbs a hill. An unmarked gravel road comes in from the left; this is labeled Point A on the map. Continue on Echo Trail as indicated by the Echo Trail sign. The trail forks in 200 yards; take the left fork and continue on Echo

Trail. The trail levels out and becomes very scenic as it passes through a thick grove of ponderosa pines and white firs. You'll cross a wash before coming to another junction and a trail sign. Go NE (left) at the junction. In 100 yards, you'll see a wooden fence and steps leading down to a paved parking area. Go down the steps, turn north (left), and follow the paved road (State Route 157) to Echo Drive. Walk along Echo Drive 200 yards to the parking area.

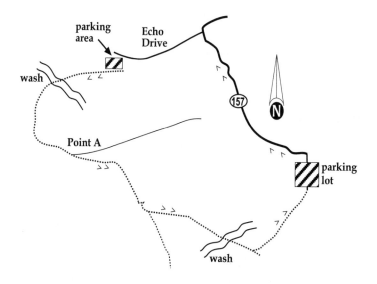

♦ ♦ ♦

Echo Overlook

Hike: Echo Overlook — up and back
Trailhead: Cathedral Rock Temporary Trail/Echo Trail — marked
Distance: 1.5 miles — round trip
Elevation gain: 473 feet
Elevation peak: 8,173 feet
Time: 1 hour
Difficulty: 3
Danger level: 2
How easy to follow: 2
Children: no
Topo map: Charleston Peak, NEV

Directions: Take U.S. 95 to State Route 157. Go left on 157 and drive 20.6 miles. Turn right onto Echo Drive at the hairpin curve. Drive 200 yards and turn left into a gravel parking area.

Overview: Echo **Trail** heads west, then SE, before a **path** veers west up a very steep slope to the overlook.

Comments: The overlook offers a great view of the Mt. Charleston Lodge and the homes on Echo Drive. Don't let the short distance fool you; the path, which is easy to follow, is one of the steepest in the Mt. Charleston Area. Photo 1 shows the trailhead sign and the overlook.

The Hike: The trail starts at the Echo Trail sign and weaves through aspens as it heads due west toward a wash. Across the wash, a trail sign indicates distances to various locations. The wide trail turns SE as it climbs a hill. An unmarked gravel road comes in from the left as an Echo Trail sign directs you to the right. In 200 yards the trail comes to a fork. The continuation of Echo Trail veers left; however, you should follow the path that veers right.

Although this path has no official name, I call it the Echo Overlook Path. It starts off with a moderate incline and heads west as the incline increases. To your left looms the sheer wall of Cathedral Rock. You'll pass a huge ponderosa pine that stands on the left side of the trail. Part of the tree's trunk has been burned. Just beyond the pine the path splits, then rejoins in a few yards. The last 100 yards are extremely steep and slippery as you climb up a slope. At the top of the slope, the path veers north (right) and concludes at the overlook.

Photo 1

Looking north, you'll see the trailhead, Cockscomb Ridge, and Mummy Mountain. To the east is Mt. Charleston Lodge.

To Descend: Retrace your steps. Be very careful as you descend the slope.

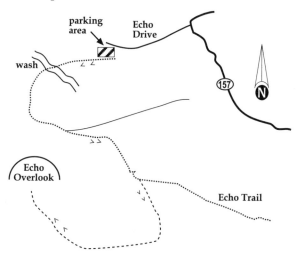

◆ ◆ ◆

Mummy's Toe

Hike: Mummy's Toe — up and back
Trailhead: State Route 158 — marked
Distance: 8 miles — round trip
Elevation gain: 2,591 feet
Elevation peak: 10,925 feet
Time: 5 to 6 hours
Difficulty: 4
Danger level: 3
How easy to follow: 5
Children: no
Topo map: Charleston Peak, NEV

Directions: Take U.S. 95 to State Route 157. Turn left on 157, drive 17.7 miles, and turn right onto State Route 158. Travel 5 miles to the North Loop trailhead sign, which is located on the west (left) side of the road. (See Photo 1.)

Overview: You'll head up the North Loop **Trail** to Mummy Springs. From there, it's a strenuous one-mile **route** to the top of Mummy's Toe.

Comments: This is another peak that few have climbed. Be careful when descending above Mummy Springs, as it's easy to send rocks tumbling down on hikers resting there.

The Hike: The trail starts off at an easy grade, wandering past ponderosa pines, pinion pines, and mountain mahogany trees. From June through September, a number of colorful flowers dot the landscape. The trail has a few moderate switchbacks before reaching a plateau. Pause at the plateau for a good view to the NE. Several bristlecone pines are scattered throughout this area, indicating that you're above 9,000 feet.

After 12 moderately steep switchbacks, the trail climbs to its highest elevation (10,200 feet). It then descends 150 feet over the next one-third mile. Catch glimpses of

Photo 1

Mummy Mountain by looking west through the trees. The limestone cliffs of Mummy's Toe hover directly in front of the trail. (See Photo 2.)

Finally, you come to Raintree, the giant and ancient bristlecone pine. It's amazing to think that when this living plant was a seedling, the Roman Empire was still centuries in the future. A wooden sign next to Raintree indicates your options and distances. Turn right and follow the trail a half-mile to Mummy Springs.

From Mummy Springs, follow a path south up the slope. (See Photo 3.) When the path veers right, don't follow it; in-

Photo 2

Photo 3

Photo 4

stead, continue south (160 degrees) straight up the slope. You'll scramble 60 yards up the extremely steep slope (class II) to the outcroppings. Use the outcroppings to scramble up another 50 yards to a wall that's directly in front of you. At the wall, go right (270 degrees) and hike 50 yards up the slope along the base of the wall. You'll go under a log that leans against the wall. As the wall curves to the right, follow it. (See Photo 4.)

Once around the wall, you'll see another larger wall up the slope about 70 yards away. Follow this wall with your eyes to the west (right), where it juts out down the slope. This is your next destination. A large cairn sits at this spot. Head SW (230 degrees) up the slope. Once you're at the cairn, you'll pass an outcropping to your right. (See Photo 5.)

Hike near the base of the wall (210 degrees) to the dry wash. It's about 100 yards from the outcropping in Photo 5 to the dry

Photo 5

wash. (See Photo 6.) A large bristlecone pine stands in the middle of the dry wash, and large logs lie at the bottom. Climb this class III wash to the bristlecone pine, head left along a ledge, then continue up an angled face. At the top of the wash, about 70 yards up the slope, lies another wall that runs east to west. Hike SE (150-160 degrees) to the wall. Go left along the wall, passing numerous cairns, and follow the wall until it ends. Turn right (150 degrees) and hike 100 yards up to the saddle. Once at the saddle, take a break and look south for a good view of Kyle Canyon. To the SE towers Mummy's Toe.

Head around the east (left) side of Mummy's Toe to avoid its face and scramble up the talus slope to the top. (See Photo 7.) Near the top, a path forms and leads to the cairn; inside the cairn is a tin box containing a sign-in register. The views from Mummy's Toe are fantastic: To the south are Kyle Canyon, Red Rock, and Las Vegas; to the west is Charleston Peak; and to the NW is Mummy Mountain.

Photo 6

To Descend: Begin by descending to the saddle. From the saddle head 100 yards north down the slope. If you start to cliff out, head west (left) to where the slope is gentle. Descend to the wall that runs east to west. It's marked with numerous cairns. Hike west along the wall 50 yards. Follow the cairns; they mark the 40-yard descent past numerous logs to the class III wash. (See Photo 6.) Once down the wash, head NE down into a drainage and follow it to Mummy Springs. Follow the trail at Mummy Springs a third of a mile to a junction. Go left onto the North Loop Trail and hike 3 miles to the trailhead.

Photo 7

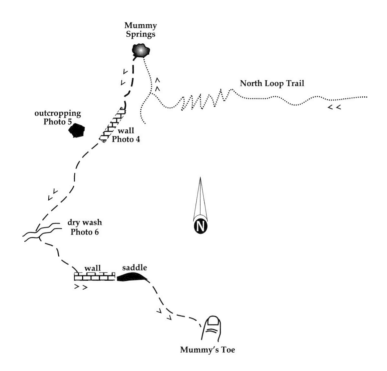

Mummy
Springs

North Loop Trail

< <

outcropping
Photo 5

wall
Photo 4

N

dry wash
Photo 6

wall   saddle

> >

Mummy's Toe

◆ ◆ ◆

Highway 158

Hike: Highway 158 — up and back
Trailhead: End of gravel road off State Route 158 — not marked
Distance: 1 mile — round trip
Elevation gain: 500 feet
Elevation peak: none
Time: 30 to 45 minutes
Difficulty: 2
Danger level: 1
How easy to follow: 1
Children: yes
Topo map: Charleston Peak, NEV

Directions: Take U.S. 95 to State Route 157. Turn left on 157, drive 17.7 miles, and make a right onto State Route 158. Travel 6.9 miles and watch for a paved pullout and a "National Forest Overlook" sign on the right side of the road. Turn left onto a secluded gravel road. The road dead-ends in 75 yards; boulders block the way. If you pass the 7-mile marker on State Route 158, you've gone too far.

Overview: The trail follows an abandoned road that heads toward Mummy's Nose.

Comments: This is a short hike with enough incline to make it a tough workout if it's done at a fast pace.

The Hike: The unmarked trailhead starts at the boulder-blocked gravel road. Hike south toward Mummy's Nose. For the first 50 yards, the road is hard to follow, but it soon becomes more defined. When it divides, take the left fork. The incline increases as the road winds between white firs and ponderosa pines. Soon after passing some burned trees, you'll come to a fork. Choose either path; they meet up again in 50 yards. This is the stopping point. The road continues for another half-mile before it ends in the middle of a forest.

To Descend: Retrace your steps.

♦ ♦ ♦

Ridge Route

Hike: Ridge Route — closed loop
Trailhead: End of gravel road off State Route 158 —
not marked
Distance: 1.5 miles — round trip
Elevation gain: 360 feet
Elevation peak: none
Time: 1 to 1.5 hours
Difficulty: 2
Danger level: 1
How easy to follow: 2
Children: yes
Topo map: Charleston Peak, NEV

Directions: Take U.S. 95 to State Route 157. Turn left on 157, drive 17.7 miles, and make a right onto State Route 158. Travel 6.9 miles and watch for a paved pullout and a "National Forest Overlook" sign on the right side of the road. Turn left onto a secluded gravel road. The road dead-ends in 75 yards; boulders block the way. If you pass the 7-mile marker on State Route 158, you've gone too far.

Overview: The **trail** follows a gravel road, then changes into a **route** when it joins an abandoned road and goes up the ridgeline. The route then descends a slope back to the gravel road.

Comments: This is a good hike to test your navigational skills. The second part of the hike is a cross-country trek up and along a ridge. You'll descend the far side of the ridge using the gravel road as a landmark.

The Hike: The unmarked trail begins just beyond the boulders that sit on the west (right) side of the odd-shaped parking area. In 30 yards you'll head west (right) on a gravel road. The slight incline makes the hiking easy as you parallel State Route 158. When

Photo 1

the gravel road turns SW, you'll get your first view of Mummy's Nose—it's an awesome sight.

In less than a half-mile, the road splits; take the left fork. The road descends and heads straight for Mummy's Nose. At the end of the descent, the road curves right; however, follow the abandoned road that continues straight (SSW) along a drainage. Photo 1 shows the abandoned road as the gravel road curves right.

The moderate incline along the abandoned road is more difficult than the first part of the hike. A fallen tree lies across the road; go into the drainage to pass it. The road narrows and becomes more defined as it weaves between the ponderosa pines and white firs. It heads SW before ending at a group of white firs. Go left and descend into the drainage that veers left (Photo 2).

Hike up the steep drainage. Near the top of the drainage, you can veer left onto a path; it's less steep than following the drainage to the ridgeline. However, you can go either way. Once you reach the ridgeline, head NE (left) and stay on the ridgeline. You'll see a saddle and a small hill in front of you; head toward them. At the top of the hill, descend the north side toward the gravel road. Look down to the low part

Photo 2

of the terrain and you'll see the gravel road. Looking beyond the road, you'll see white outcroppings; they should be on your left. When you reach the road, go right and follow it back to the trailhead.

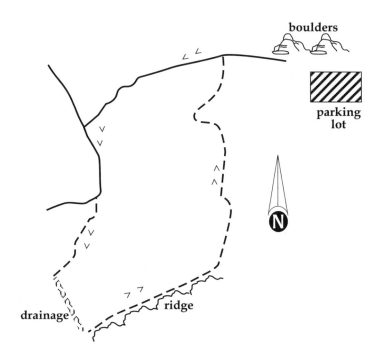

♦ ♦ ♦

Desert Overlook

Hike: Desert Overlook — up and back
Trailhead: End of gravel road off State Route 158 —
not marked
Distance: 1 mile — round trip
Elevation gain: 158 feet
Elevation peak: 8,432 feet
Time: 30 to 60 minutes
Difficulty: 1
Danger level: 1
How easy to follow: 2
Children: yes
Topo map: Charleston Peak, NEV

Directions: Take U.S. 95 to State Route 157. Turn left on 157, drive 17.7 miles, and make a right onto State Route 158. Travel 6.9 miles and watch for a paved pullout and a "National Forest Overlook" sign on the right side of the road. Turn left onto a secluded gravel road. The road dead-ends in 75 yards; boulders block the way. If you pass the 7-mile marker on State Route 158, you've gone too far.

Overview: The **trail** follows a gravel road and forks right, leading to the overlook.

Comments: This is a good hike for beginners and children. It takes little effort to reach the overlook, and the view it offers is surprisingly nice.

The Hike: The unmarked trail begins just beyond the boulders that sit on the west (right) side of the odd-shaped parking area.

In 30 yards you'll head west (right) on the gravel road. The slight incline makes the hiking easy as you parallel State Route 158. When the gravel road turns SW, you'll get your first view of Mummy's Nose—it's an awesome sight.

Photo 1

In less than a half-mile the road splits; take the right fork. The fork heads NNE and ends in 75 yards; however, a path lies approximately 30 yards ahead. To find the path, continue in the same direction (NNE), weaving between the trees. Look for the large boulder (Photo 1); the path lies in front of it. Take a left at the path. Fifteen yards past the boulder, turn right and walk up and over the rock (class I). Pick up the path just beyond the bushes and go left; it's about 75 yards to the overlook. The overlook offers a good view of the desert floor to the right and Mack's Peak to the left.

To Descend: Retrace your steps, making sure to turn left at the main gravel road.

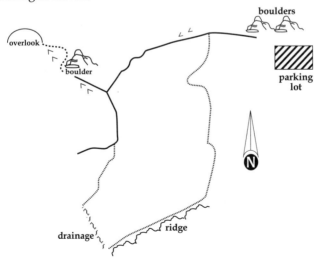

The Sisters

Hike: The Sisters (South and North) — closed loop
Trailhead: End of Mack's Canyon Road — not marked
Distance: 7 miles — round trip
Elevation gain: 1,482 feet
Elevation peak: 10,175 feet and 10,040 feet
Time: 6 to 7 hours
Difficulty: 4
Danger level: 5
How easy to follow: 5
Children: no
Topo map: Charleston Peak, NEV

Directions: Take U.S. 95 to State Route 156. Go left on 156, drive 14.2 miles, and turn right onto Mack's Canyon Road. If you pass the intersection of 158/156, you've gone too far. Follow the gravel road until it dead-ends (4.3 miles).

Overview: The **route** follows a spring and climbs to a ridgeline; you'll traverse it for the final scramble to the South Sister. From there, it's tricky as you go along the east side to the west side of South Sister. You'll then hike along the west side of the North Sister and climb the chute to the ridge that leads to the peak.

Comments: This is one of the best hikes in Mt. Charleston. You'll begin by hiking along a spring, then following a route that takes you through two rock arches and past two caves. Both Sisters offer great views of Lee Canyon. The elevation gain is greater than stated because of the descent from South Sister and the ascent to North Sister.

North Sister ↓ **South Sister** ↓

Photo 1

The Hike: The unmarked trail begins by the boulder-blocked gravel road. The grade is easy as the gravel road heads south. Soon the South Sister comes into view. The road turns into a path as it crosses an unnamed, year-round spring. The incline increases, but the pain is offset by the lush greenery in the area. The path goes up a steep incline and intersects another path; go right. In 50 yards the path disappears as the hike turns into a cross-country route. Head north up the slope to the ridgeline.

Once on the ridgeline, you can see the South Sister, which lies SE. A path begins on the ridgeline and heads east toward the South Sister. There are only a few steep sections along the ridgeline. Great vistas of Charleston, Griffith, McFarland, and Mack's peaks are visible during this part of the hike. The road below to the south is Old Mill Road. The South Sister lies 60 degrees to the NE. (See Photo 1.)

The route crosses a saddle before making the final climb to the base of South Sister. A faint path leads to the base. This is the hardest part of the hike. (See the white line in Photo 2 for an overview of the route.) At the saddle go left and climb the chute that leads to the peak. (See Photo 3.) At the top of the chute, go left again and scramble to the peak. A sign-in book in a cairn marks the summit. The footing is narrow along the peak—be careful.

Photo 2

One Sister down, one to go! Descend the same chute and go north (left) down and around to the east wall of the South Sister. Hike along the wall for 40 yards, then descend to a second, smaller wall. The 30-foot-wide sloping ledge you're walking on becomes narrow in places. Head west (left) 10 yards; you'll see a bristlecone that looks like a telephone pole (Photo 4). Scramble toward another wall.

Parallel the wall. In 50 yards, go between the wall and another bristlecone. Just past this point, you'll hike through a rock arch. After the arch, there's a break in the wall. Go

Photo 3

left, through the break, and descend the chute. You're now on the west side of the South Sister.

Once the chute ends, descend another 100 yards. To your right, a wall forms. (See Photo 5.) Hike along the wall. You'll soon pass through a magnificent, 40-foot rock arch. (See Photo 6.) Continue north along the wall. Just after the North Sister comes into view, the wall pulls away and goes up a slope. You can continue along the wall, but traversing the slope is easier. The same wall curves down about 75 yards ahead (you can't see it from this point). Head east (70 degrees) along a very faint path. When the wall comes into view, look for a log leaning against a crack in the wall. (See Photo 7). Climb through the crack (class III) to the saddle that separates South Sister and North Sister. (Photo 8 shows an overview of the route up to North Sister.) At the saddle, look east to spot a rock arch near the top of a 50-foot pinnacle. This makes a great photo.

Photo 4

Photo 5　　　　　　　**Photo 6**

The sheer walls of the North Sister are directly in front of you. From here you'll traverse the west side of the North Sister to a point where you can climb the wall. On the far side of the saddle lies an outcropping; head north (20 degrees). You should be heading left of the outcropping. Soon you'll come to a 30-foot log leaning against another outcropping. Hike to the right of it. At this point the wall starts to pull away. Go east (right) and

scramble 60 yards to the wall. Continue north along the wall. You'll pass two small caves. Beyond the caves, another outcropping juts from the wall; go down and around it. Scramble up the scree and over another outcropping. At this point you're 50 feet below the wall, heading NW. Photo 9 shows where to start your scramble toward the wall. Notice the logs in front of this outcropping. At the top of the outcropping, go east (right) and scramble up to the base of the wall. Photo 10 shows where you climb (class III) the wall.

Photo 7

At the top of the wall, the bristlecone pines are abundant as you head SE up the slope toward the peak. Climb the chute in Photo 11 (class II). You're now on a ridge that travels to the peak. Photo 12 shows the

Photo 8

100-yard route along the ridge to the peak. Veer to the right side of the ridge for the final 50-yard scramble to the peak. Remember this ridge; it's a landmark when you start your descent.

The view from the North Sister is fantastic. You can see part of the route you just hiked. State Route 156 is to the south, and across 156 are the three peaks that make up Mummy's Head. A sign-in book rests in a cairn.

To Descend: Face north and look at the ridge you just climbed. To the right of the ridge, you'll see bristlecone pines on a steep slope. This is where you'll scramble down. Be very careful not to dislodge rocks onto hikers below you.

You'll head down the steep slope until you reach the road you first hiked. Start your descent by heading NNW down the slope, keeping Mack's Peak at about the 11 o'clock position. Near the bottom of the slope, look for any of the drainages. Choose one and use it to descend to the road. By going this way, you'll avoid a final steep descent. When you reach the road, go

Photo 9

north (right) and follow it back to your car. If you descend to the path instead of the road, it's a farther walk to your car. The descent will take from 60 to 90 minutes.

Photo 10

Photo 11

Photo 12

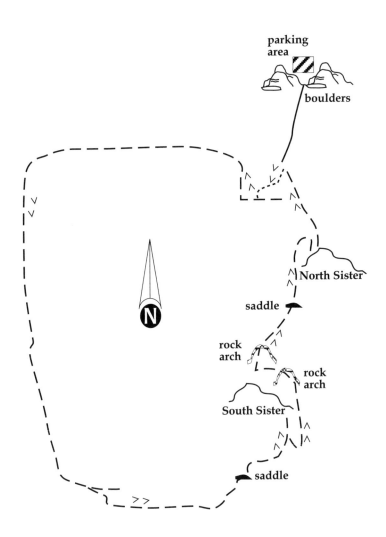

Mummy's Nose

Hike: Mummy's Nose — up and back
Trailhead: Pulloff along State Route 156 — not marked
Distance: 5 miles — round trip
Elevation gain: 2,846 feet
Elevation peak: 10,748 feet
Time: 5 to 6 hours
Difficulty: 4
Danger level: 4
How easy to follow: 4
Children: no
Topo map: Charleston Peak, NEV

Directions: Take U.S. 95 north to State Route 156. Turn left onto 156, drive 16 miles, and park at the large gravel pullout on the north (right) side of the road. The pullout is located less than a mile past the turnoff for State Route 158.

Overview: The **route** is a cross-country trek to a gully. Scramble up the drainage to the saddle. From the saddle, you'll hike up a class III chute and along the ridgeline to the peak.

Comments: With each step along the ridgeline, the views get better and better. This hike is one of my favorites at Mt. Charleston; few people have stood at this peak. Photo 1 shows Mummy's Nose as seen from State Route 156. Photo 2 shows the saddle you'll climb. During the summer, huge bumblebees inhabit the lower part of the drainage. Luckily, they prefer flowers to humans!

Photo 1   **Photo 2**

The Hike: Walk south along State Route 156. In less than 100 yards, go left onto the gravel road marked by the sign, "Toiyabe National Forest, Summer Homes, Lee Canyon." The road passes under two power lines and curves right. Along the curve, a shallow drainage comes in from the left; two stumps mark the start of the drainage. Hike up the drainage, scrambling left out of it to avoid the dense brush near the top. Once at the top, parallel the drainage until the brush clears, then drop back into it. Hike east (90 degrees) up the drainage until it disappears. In about 50 yards, you'll intersect an abandoned gravel road. Take a right at the road and follow it until you intersect a prominent gravel road less than 40 yards away. Cross the prominent gravel road— don't follow it.

Photo 3

Your next goal is a gully, which you can't see from your present position. There's a landmark to help you find the gully: a 50-foot pinnacle. An aban-

Photo 4

doned gravel road starts 60 yards before the pinnacle and travels just to the left of it. Due to the dense brush, it's difficult to see the pinnacle from a distance. You don't have to follow the road and find the pinnacle, but doing so will reassure you that you're headed toward the gully. Begin your search for the abandoned road by heading SE (120 degrees) up the slope's moderate incline. The road is about 80 to 100 yards ahead. If the slope becomes too steep, you're too far to the west (right). Once you find the road, follow it to the pinnacle. When you pass the pinnacle, leave the road and head east (100 to 110 degrees) up the slope toward the gully. Don't veer too far right (west) or you'll go into the wrong gully. When you reach the correct gully, don't hike down into it; instead, follow a faint path marked with an occasional cairn. The path parallels the gully for about a quarter-mile. Follow the path down the talus slope into a drainage located at the bottom of the gully. If you pass the craggy wall in Photo 3, you've hiked too far.

The saddle is your next destination. It lies ESE (100 degrees), almost 1,000 feet above. Start hiking up the drainage. Photo 4 shows where the drainage divides; head into the less prominent left fork. This part of the drainage is mostly class II climbing. Stay in the drainage; don't climb on either bank. You'll eventually pass a small cave to the right of the drainage. (See Photo 5.)

Photo 5

Photo 6

Just past the cave, leave the drainage to avoid the many spiny plants and climb the steep embankment along the left wall. Scramble over the smooth log at the top of the embankment and head east (100 degrees) toward the next wall (40 yards ahead). From this point to the saddle, it's easier to follow the paths that go alongside the various walls, which are to your left. Continue east toward the saddle. When you come to a wall, climb the low point in the wall (class II) and continue another 100 yards to the saddle. Take a break once you reach the saddle. To the SE lies Mummy's Toe.

The strenuous part of the hike is over. Stay on the west side of the saddle and head NE to the chute that lies 50 yards away. (See Photo 6.) Climb the chute (class III) to the 30-foot wall. Just before the wall, a ledge forms along the right. Traverse the ledge to a bluff; it offers a great view of Mummy Mountain. Climb the rocky wall on the north side of the bluff, then head toward the false peak that lies ahead (north). Climb the false peak's south (right) side. Now follow a faint path that leads to the real peak on the north (left) side of the ridgeline. The path disappears as the route goes up a rock face (class II), then resumes and leads toward the final chute seen in Photo 7. Once up the final chute, stay along the ridgeline; the views get better and better. A huge cairn marks the peak. You'll find a sign-in log in a tin

Photo 7

can inside a cairn. Count the names—there aren't many.

This peak, which few have reached, has a magical feel. The views are magnificent. To the SW lie Mummy's Chin and Mummy's Forehead; to the south rests Mummy's Tummy. If you've hiked the route to Mummy's Tummy (I covered it in *Hiking Las Vegas*), you can see the chute you climbed. The next time you're on the North Loop Trail before Raintree, look NW to see the peak you're now standing on. From that angle it looks impossible to climb.

To Descend: Follow the ridgeline south to the final chute. Continue south to the bluff. Head north on the ledge to the chute. Climb down the chute to the saddle, then head down the gully and veer to the right side. It's quicker to descend following the footsteps than hugging the north wall. Once past the cave, you'll see the gravel parking lot and the lower part of the gully. Go into the gully and look for the same path you hiked down to reach the gully. Follow the path; look for the pinnacle you passed on the way up. After you're past the pinnacle, head NW toward State Route 156. Your car is parked alongside 156 in the gravel pullout.

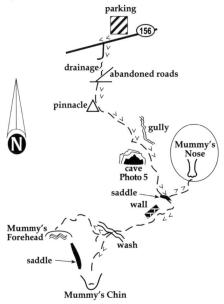

◆ ◆ ◆

Mummy's Chin

Hike: Mummy's Chin — up and back
Trailhead: Pulloff along State Route 156 — not marked
Distance: 8 miles — round trip
Elevation gain: 3,135 feet
Elevation peak: 11,037 feet
Time: 8 to 9 hours
Difficulty: 5
Danger level: 5
How easy to follow: 5
Children: no
Topo map: Charleston Peak, NEV

Directions: Take U.S. 95 north to State Route 156. Turn left onto 156, drive 16 miles, and park at the large gravel pullout on the north (right) side of the road. The pullout is located less than a mile past the turnoff for State Route 158.

Overview: The **route** is a cross-country trek to a gully. Scramble up the drainage in the gully to get to the saddle. From the saddle, descend the other side and follow the wall to a wash. Scramble up the wash to another saddle. From the saddle, ascend the scree slope to the peak.

Comments: This is another tough hike, but you'll be rewarded by bagging a peak where few have gone. Be very careful not to dislodge rocks during the descent. Photo 1 shows Mummy's Chin as you drive along State Route 156. Photo 2 shows the saddle—the halfway point in the hike.

Photo 1   **Photo 2**

The Hike: Walk south along State Route 156. In less than 100 yards, go left onto the gravel road marked by the sign, "Toiyabe National Forest, Summer Homes, Lee Canyon." The road passes under two power lines and curves right. Along the curve, a shallow drainage comes in from the left; two stumps mark the start of the drainage. Hike up the drainage, scrambling left out of it to avoid the dense brush near the top. Once at the top, parallel the

Photo 3

drainage until the brush clears, then drop back into it. Hike east (90 degrees) up the drainage until it disappears. In about 50 yards, you'll intersect an abandoned gravel road. Take a right at the road and follow it until you intersect a prominent gravel road less than 40 yards away. Cross the prominent gravel road—don't follow it.

Your next goal is a gully, which you can't see from your present position. There's a landmark to help you find the gully: a 50-foot pinnacle. An abandoned gravel road starts 60

Photo 4

yards before the pinnacle and travels just to the left of it. Due to the dense brush, it's difficult to see the pinnacle from a distance. You don't have to follow the road and find the pinnacle, but doing so will reassure you that you're headed toward the gully. Begin your search for the abandoned road by heading SE (120 degrees) up the slope's moderate incline. The road is about 80 to 100 yards ahead. If the slope becomes too steep, you're too far to the west (right). Once you find the road, follow it to the pinnacle. When you pass the pinnacle, leave the road and head east (100 to 110 degrees) up the slope toward the gully. Don't veer too far right (west) or you'll go into the wrong gully. When you reach the correct gully, don't hike down into it; instead, follow a faint path marked with an occasional cairn. The path parallels the gully for about a quarter-mile. Follow the path down the talus slope into a drainage located at the bottom of the gully. If you pass the craggy wall in Photo 3, you've hiked too far.

The saddle is your next destination. It lies ESE (100 degrees), almost 1,000 feet above. Start hiking up the drainage. Photo 4 shows where the drainage divides; head into the less prominent left fork. This part of the drainage is mostly class II climbing. Stay in the drainage; don't climb on either bank. You'll eventually pass a small cave to the right of the drainage. (See Photo 5.) Just

Photo 5

Mummy's Chin

Photo 6

past the cave, leave the drainage to avoid the many spiny plants and climb the steep embankment along the left wall. Scramble over the smooth log at the top of the embankment and head east (100 degrees) toward the next wall (40 yards ahead). From this point to the saddle, it's easier to follow the paths that go alongside the various walls, which are to your left. Continue east toward the saddle. When you come to a wall, climb the low point in the wall (class II) and continue another 100 yards to the saddle. Take a break once you reach the saddle. To the SE lies Mummy's Toe.

The next section of the hike traverses the base of a 150-foot-high wall to a dry wash. Start by hiking SSE down the other side of the saddle. Follow the wall as it curves right. The terrain flattens as you head SSW (200 degrees.) Photo 6 shows the wall and Mummy's Chin. Soon you'll go through an arch formed by a twisted bristlecone. This is a great photo opportunity. The wall descends slightly as you pass between it and a dead bristlecone. Stay next to the wall during this part of the hike. Eventually, you'll leave the wall and traverse south, passing the bottom edge of a smaller wall. The traverse is tough, but only 50 yards. (See Photo 7.) Once past the smaller wall, continue south 100 yards to the dry wash.

Scramble SW up the wash. (See Photo 8.) To avoid the spiny plants halfway up the wash, hike on the faint path along the wash's left side. Photo 9 shows the class III climb up the wash. Just above this point, the wash divides. Take the left fork and scramble up the class III wash. (See

Photo 7

Photo 10.) After the wash ends, continue SW (220 degrees) up the limestone to a saddle that lies between Mummy's Chin and Mummy's Forehead. From the saddle you can see Ski Lee below to the SW. If you're looking at Ski Lee, Mummy's Chin is to the south (left).

The saddle lies only a few minutes from the peak. Go south (left) about 50 yards, descend around the jutting wall, then climb the scree slope (class II) to the peak. (See Photo 11.)

Photo 8

A sign-in book is inside a cairn. The view from the peak is awesome. To the north lies Mummy's Nose. About 200 yards to the NW stands Mummy's Forehead, the highest of these three peaks. To the SE sits Mummy's Tummy.

To Descend: Descend the scree slope and the limestone until you reach the top of the wash; climb down it. When you're on the same level as the base of the 150-foot-high wall you traversed earlier, leave the wash. Follow the wall back to the

saddle, then head down the gully and veer to the right side. It's quicker to descend following the footsteps than it is to hug the north wall. Once past the cave, you'll see the gravel parking lot and the lower part of the gully. Go into the gully and look for the same path you hiked down to reach the gully. Follow the path; look for the pinnacle you passed on the way up. After you're past the pinnacle, head NW toward State Route 156. Your car is parked alongside 156 in the gravel pullout.

Photo 9

Photo 10

Photo 11

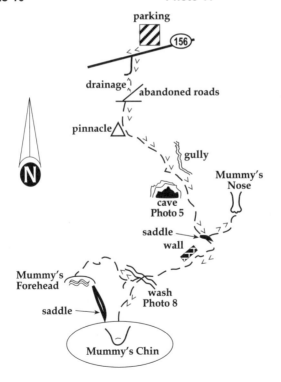

◆ ◆ ◆

Mummy's Forehead

Hike: Mummy's Forehead — up and back
Trailhead: Pulloff along State Route 156 — not marked
Distance: 8 miles — round trip
Elevation gain: 3,138 feet
Elevation peak: 11,040 feet
Time: 6 to 8 hours
Difficulty: 5
Danger level: 5
How easy to follow: 5
Children: no
Topo map: Charleston Peak, NEV

Directions: Take U.S. 95 north to State Route 156. Turn left onto 156, drive 16 miles, and park at the large gravel pullout on the north (right) side of the road. The pullout is located less than a mile past the turnoff for State Route 158.

Overview: The **route** is a cross-country trek to a gully. Scramble up the drainage in the gully to the saddle. From the saddle, descend the other side and follow the wall to the wash. Scramble up the wash to a series of chutes that leads to the peak.

Comments: This is a tough hike, but you'll be able to stand on a peak that few people have stood on before. You'll see bristlecone pines twisted into unbelievable shapes; you'll even walk through an archway of bristlecone. Photo 1 shows Mummy's Forehead as seen from State Route 156. Photo 2 shows the saddle—the halfway point in the hike.

Caution: Due to loose rock, limit your group to four people.

Photo 1

Photo 2

The Hike: Walk south along State Route 156. In less than 100 yards, go left onto the gravel road marked by the sign, "Toiyabe National Forest, Summer Homes, Lee Canyon." The road passes under two power lines and curves right. Along the curve, a shallow drainage comes in from the left; two stumps mark the start of the drainage. Hike up the drainage, scrambling left out of it to avoid the dense brush near the top. Once at the top, parallel the drainage until the brush clears, then drop back into it. Hike east (90 degrees) up the drainage until it disappears. In about 50 yards, you'll intersect an abandoned gravel road. Take a right at the road and follow it until you intersect a prominent gravel road less than 40 yards away. Cross the prominent gravel road—don't follow it.

Photo 3

Your next goal is a gully, which you can't see from your present position. There's a landmark to help you find the gully: a 50-foot pinnacle. An aban-

Photo 4

doned gravel road starts 60 yards before the pinnacle and travels just to the left of it. Due to the dense brush, it's difficult to see the pinnacle from a distance. You don't have to follow the road and find the pinnacle, but doing so will reassure you that you're headed toward the gully. Begin your search for the abandoned road by heading SE (120 degrees) up the slope's moderate incline. The road is about 80 to 100 yards ahead. If the slope becomes too steep, you're too far to the west (right). Once you find the road, follow it to the pinnacle. When you pass the pinnacle, leave the road and head east (100 to 110 degrees) up the slope toward the gully. Don't veer too far right (west) or you'll go into the wrong gully. When you reach the correct gully, don't hike down into it; instead, follow a faint path marked with an occasional cairn. The path parallels the gully for about a quarter-mile. Follow the path down the talus slope into a drainage located at the bottom of the gully. If you pass the craggy wall in Photo 3, you've hiked too far.

The saddle is your next destination. It lies ESE (100 degrees), almost 1,000 feet above. Start hiking up the drainage. Photo 4 shows where the drainage divides; head into the less prominent left fork. This part of the drainage is mostly class II climbing. Stay in the drainage; don't climb on either bank. You'll eventually pass a

Photo 5

Photo 6

small cave to the right of the drainage. (See Photo 5.) Just past the cave, leave the drainage to avoid the many spiny plants and climb the steep embankment along the left wall. Scramble over the smooth log at the top of the embankment and head east (100 degrees) toward the next wall (40 yards ahead). From this point to the saddle, it's easier to follow the paths that go alongside the various walls, which are to your left. Continue east toward the saddle. When you come to a wall, climb the low point in the wall (class II) and continue another 100 yards to the saddle. Take a break once you reach the saddle. To the SE lies Mummy's Toe.

The next section of the hike traverses the base of a 150-foot-high wall to a dry wash. Start by hiking SSE down the other side of the saddle. Follow the wall as it curves right. The terrain flattens as you head SSW (200 degrees.) Photo 6 shows the wall and Mummy's Chin. Soon you'll go through an arch formed by a twisted bristlecone. This is a great photo opportunity. The wall descends slightly as you pass between it and a dead bristlecone. Stay next to the wall during this part of the hike. Eventually, you'll leave the wall and traverse south, passing the bottom edge of a smaller wall. The traverse is tough, but only 50 yards. (See Photo 7.) Once past the smaller wall, continue south 100 yards to the dry wash.

Scramble SW up the wash. (See Photo 8.) To avoid the spiny plants halfway up the wash, hike on the faint path along the wash's left side. Photo 9 shows the class III climb up

Photo 7

Photo 8

the wash. Just above this point, the wash divides. Head into the right fork; the left fork goes up to Mummy's Chin. A huge log marks the start of this strenuous trek. Above the log, the wash fades as it becomes a scree slope filled with pine cones. (See Photo 10.)

Notice the bristlecone that leans to the right (Photo 10). It's left of a group of tall bristlecones, about 80 yards from the huge log. Scramble to this bristlecone. About 30 yards past it, there's a 15-foot-high, 40-foot-long wall. At the right side of the wall is a scree chute. Look for a large cairn. This is the beginning of a series of chutes that will take you to the peak. (Be sure to look for the cairns that mark the route through the chutes.) Scramble up the scree chute to the white-colored wall in Photo 11.

When you reach the wall, go left. The terrain levels out temporarily, and you'll pass a bristlecone that has twisted itself into a circle. Use the wall to help you scramble up the steep scree slope. Photo 12 shows the wall and scree chute above the

Photo 9

Photo 10

twisted bristlecone. As you near the top of the slope, it's easier to veer left and scramble up any of the chutes to the top.

Photo 11

The hard part is over! From here, head west (left) 100 yards along the ridge to the peak. The moderate incline will seem easy after what you've just climbed. To the west are Mack's Peak and McFarland Peak. To the SW 2,000 feet below sits Ski Lee, a popular ski area. About 200 yards south is Mummy's Chin. Mummy's Tummy, the main part of Mummy Mountain, is farther south. Look for a sign-in book inside a cairn. As you'll see, there's a lot to explore up here, unless the weather is stormy and lightning and thunder discourage you.

To Descend: Retrace your steps by heading NE toward Mummy's Nose, the gray-colored peak. Look for a cairn on a stump that marks the top of the chutes you just climbed. Be careful not to dislodge rocks while descending the chutes. Look for the twisted circular bristlecone. Once out of the chutes, go down the scree slope into the wash. When you're on the same level as the base of the 150-foot wall you traversed earlier, leave the wash. Follow the wall back to the saddle, then head down the gully and veer to the right side. It's quicker to descend following the footsteps than it is to hug the

Photo 12

north wall. Once past the cave, you'll see the gravel parking lot and the lower part of the gully. Go into the gully and look for the same path you hiked down to reach the gully. Follow the path; look for the pinnacle you passed on the way up. After you're past the pinnacle, head NW toward State Route 156. Your car is parked alongside 156 in the gravel pullout.

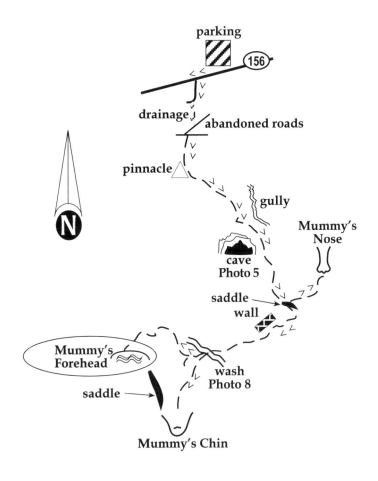

◆ ◆ ◆

McFarland Peak

Hike: McFarland Peak — up and back
Trailhead: Gravel road off of Cold Creek Road —
not marked
Distance: 8 miles — round trip
Elevation gain: 3,592 feet
Elevation peak: 10,742 feet
Time: 6 to 8 hours
Difficulty: 4
Danger level: 4
How easy to follow: 4
Children: no
Topo map: Charleston Peak, NEV

Directions: From Las Vegas, take U.S. 95 north 19 miles past
the turnoff for State Route 157 to Cold Creek Road. Turn west
(left) onto the signed Cold Creek Road. Travel 9.6 miles and
turn south (left) onto the *first* gravel road. Drive 5.3 miles and
park at the divide, which is not very obvious. (See Photo 1.)
Do not drive down the right fork of the gravel road; your vehicle functions as a landmark if it's parked at the divide. A
high-clearance vehicle is recommended.

Overview: The **route** goes across the desert and through the
woods to locally named North Canyon. It then heads south up
North Canyon to the summit ridge and follows the ridge SW to
the peak.

Comments: This is the best route to the seldom-climbed
McFarland Peak, as it avoids the 5-mile approach hike on the
Bonanza Trail. The views along the summit ridge are awesome.

Photo 1

Warning: Do *not* attempt this hike if it looks like rain.

The Hike: The crux of the route is finding North Canyon, which lies just below the tan-colored cliff circled in Photo 1. (Photo 2 is a close-up of the cliff.) Although from the trailhead the cliff looks easy to locate, once you're in the woods, you lose sight of it.

To begin your cross-country trek, hike SW down the steep gravel road and up the other side, then head SSW through the burnt area (the result of a fire many years ago) toward North Canyon. There's an opening and a faint path to follow through the woods. The path is reasonably clear of brush, though you'll need to watch for low-hanging branches. Your bearing is 205 degrees. The path drops into a shallow drainage and continues south. If you start traversing a slope, you're too far to the east (left). When you see the tan-colored cliff to your right, you're in North Canyon. Continue south on the path; it becomes easier to follow as you hike deeper into the canyon.

When the drainage divides, take the right fork, which stays near the west (right) wall of the canyon. About an hour from

Photo 2

the trailhead, the canyon walls tighten and the grade increases. This section of the route is mostly class II. Climb the wall (class III) shown in Photo 3. If you want to avoid the wall, head east (left) around it. Past the wall, long slabs of limestone line the bottom of the drainage. Beyond the slabs, the terrain flattens and the summit ridge comes into view. When the drainage comes to a three-way divide, continue south (straight) in the shallow drainage, which becomes more distinct in 50 yards. Two cairns mark the divide.

Photo 3

From the three-way divide, hike about 250 yards up the rocky drainage until it bends to the west (right). A cairn sits on a large boulder at this spot. Head SE (don't follow the drainage to the right) up the bank of the drainage. (See Photo 4.) At the top of the bank, the drainage resumes and heads SE toward the summit ridge. It's a steep trek up the drainage. When it fades, continue SE another 150 yards to the summit ridge. Depending on where you intersect the ridge, you might need to head west away from it and up through a notch before you can see the final part of the summit ridge, as shown in Photo 5.

This detour avoids the exposed class III or class IV climb along the ridge.

From the notch it's a 400-yard trek to the peak. For an awesome sight, walk east to the edge of the summit ridge; it's more than 500 feet to the bottom. The rugged mountain to the NE is Mack's Peak. Follow the summit ridge SW to McFarland Peak. Due to exposure along the ridge, it's quicker and safer to hike slightly west of the ridge. You'll pass two low-angle limestone ramps that lead to the ridge. The peak is at

Photo 4

the top of the second ramp.

Photo 5

A small cairn, which contains a register, sits at the peak. You'll enjoy a spectacular 360-degree view from the peak. Looking north, you can see Bonanza Peak and Willow Peak; to the east are Mack's Peak and the Sisters; to the south lie Mummy Mountain and Charleston Peak; and way out to the west, on a clear day, you can see the snow-capped Sierras.

To Descend: Scramble down the limestone slab and head 400 yards NE, paralleling the summit ridge. Hike through the notch and go NW 150 yards down the slope into the drainage. Follow the drainage down to the class III wall (Photo 3); go around to the east (right) of the wall to get down if necessary. Continue in the drainage and follow the path when the terrain levels. Look west (left) for the tan-colored cliff (see Photo 2). At this point you'll be in the woods. Stay in or near the drainage and follow the path; your overall bearing is NNE (25 degrees). Once out of the woods, you can see your vehicle by looking NNE (30 degrees).

SOUTHERN NEVADA
♦ ADVANCED ADVENTURES ♦

The adventures in this section are all classic hikes near Las Vegas. Many locals have heard of the four peaks covered here but have never stood on these summits. Hayford Peak, an all-day hike, is the highest peak in the Sheep Mountain Range. Also in the Sheep Mountains, Gass Peak looks straight down on Las Vegas from the north. La Madre Peak hovers over the Red Rock Peaks and offers one of the best views of Red Rock Canyon and Las Vegas. Mt. Potosi, southwest of Las Vegas, is distinguishable by the numerous antennas at its summit.

As a reminder, the hikes to Hayford Peak, Gass Peak, La Madre Peak, and Mt. Potosi are all advanced and should be undertaken by experienced hikers only.

◆ ◆ ◆

La Madre Peak

Hike: La Madre Peak — up and back
Trailhead: End of Road 214 — not marked
Distance: 7 miles — round trip
Elevation gain: 3,354 feet
Elevation peak: 8,154 feet
Time: 5 to 6 hours
Difficulty: 4
Danger level: 3
How easy to follow: 3
Children: no
Topo map: La Madre Mtn., NEV

Directions: From the intersection of West Charleston and Rampart boulevards, head west on West Charleston 4.2 miles and turn right onto an unmarked dirt road. (The dirt road is across from the end of the water containment basin.) At 2.8 miles the dirt road divides; go left. When the road divides again at 4.1 miles, turn right. At 4.5 miles, you'll see an iron gate. Park here; this marks where the hike begins. A high-clearance vehicle is necessary.

Overview: The **route** follows a jeep road NW to the base of the mountain, then it's a steep trek NW up to a saddle. From there, the route travels NE along the slope to the peak.

Comments: Although this hike starts at the edge of Red Rock Canyon, the terrain is limestone and scree. La Madre Peak offers one of the best 360-degree views of any peak in the Spring Mountains. Be careful not to dislodge rocks onto fellow hikers when descending. Photo 1 shows an overview of the route.

The Hike: Head west along the jeep road. The incline is slight, but you'll sink into the sand, making it difficult to walk. In about a mile the road divides; take the right fork. In less than 100 yards the road divides again (you should see a yel-

La Madre Peak

Photo 1

low sign embedded in a rock at this fork). Go left. The road becomes steep as it heads NW toward the base of the mountain. Less than 3 miles from the trailhead, the road ends. From here, head NW up the steep slope and around the right side of the wall that lies ahead. (See Photo 2.)

It's a steep cross-country trek to the north (right) side of the wall. You'll cross two small drainages. Once you're on the slope, follow a faint path toward the notch, which lies 50 yards from the wall's right corner. (See Photo 3.) Descend the notch and follow the path up the steep gully. Look for cairns along the way. The path stays near the wall as it winds toward the saddle.

At the saddle, head NE (right) toward the peak. At this point the peak is less than a half-mile away, but you still have more than 500 feet to gain. There's no path to follow; however, the direction of travel (NE) is obvious. A faint path appears during the last 50 yards to the peak. A small cairn, which contains a sign-in book, marks the summit. The few signatures in the book prove that not too many hikers reach this peak. The views from La Madre are some of the best in Southern Nevada. To the NW

Wall

Photo 2

Photo 3

stands Griffith Peak and Mummy Mountain. Red Rock Canyon is SE, and if you look east, you'll see Las Vegas. On a clear day you can even see Lake Mead and the Muddy Mountains.

To Descend: Head SE back to the saddle. Follow the path down the gully. Once on the slope, you can see the jeep road below. Follow the road back to the trailhead.

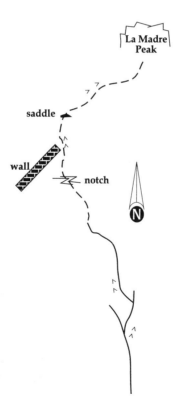

◆ ◆ ◆

Potosi Mountain

Hike: Potosi Mountain — up and back
Trailhead: Potosi Springs — not marked
Distance: 9 miles — round trip
Elevation gain: 2,249 feet
Elevation peak: 8,514 feet
Time: 6 to 8 hours
Difficulty: 4
Danger level: 2
How easy to follow: 5
Children: no
Topo map: Potosi Mtn., NEV

Directions: Drive south on I-15 and take the Blue Diamond Highway (State Route 160) exit at Silverton Casino. Head west on State Route 160. About 14 miles beyond the intersection of Rainbow Boulevard, turn left onto a gravel road marked by a sign that reads, "Potosi Mtn.—BSA Camp." Drive 4.3 miles (never turning off the main road) to a rectangular, chainlink fence in a large open area on the left. On the right sits an A-frame building. Park near the chainlink fence. This area is known as Potosi Springs.

Overview: The **route** gains the ridgeline and follows it eastward to the peak.

Comments: The peak offers fantastic views of Las Vegas and Red Rock Canyon. There's a path, but it's hard to follow. The two antennas at the peak serve as landmarks and are visible along much of the route.

Photo 1

The Hike: The hike starts off strenuous as you head SE along an old gravel road. (See Photo 1.) In 200 yards you'll see Potosi Mine. Go left onto the path that starts just before the mine. The path zigzags NE up the steep slope. Soon you'll come to an outcropping and a ventilation shaft for the mine. Go left onto the path. The hikers in Photo 2 are past the ventilation shaft and are heading NE up the ridgeline to a spot where the slope flattens (about 100 yards).

Follow the path up the ridgeline to another ridgeline that runs north to south. Once on the north/south ridgeline, you'll see two antennas at the peak. On your right is a burned area, which you'll use as a landmark during your descent. Head NE (left) along the ridgeline and follow the path. This part of the route is less strenuous. The hikers in Photo 3 are heading

Photo 2

NE toward the top of the sheer wall. Once at the sheer wall, you'll see Red Rock Canyon to the left.

The path becomes steep as it follows the ridgeline up the slope. When the terrain levels, you'll see the two antennas again. Photo 4 was taken along the ridgeline. The views of Las Vegas and Red Rock Canyon are fantastic from this vantage point.

Eventually you'll see a saddle that lies about 100 feet below. There are many ways to climb down to the saddle; the easiest is described here. As you start to descend, go right and follow the path as it hugs a wall. The path makes a sharp left and heads toward the chute in Photo 5. At the bottom of the chute, the path heads south for about 15 yards, then turns east (left) toward the saddle. Two large

Photo 3

wooden poles with wires strung from them stand at the saddle.

From the saddle, the idea is to hike the ridgeline that travels along the top of the highest wall. Follow the path that starts at the saddle for about 100 yards. Watch for the large boulders on the left of the path. About 15 yards past the boulders, leave the main path and head east (100 degrees) along an obscure path. Aim for the antennas. When the slope flattens, stay along the ridgeline. You'll be walking on top of the wall.

Photo 6 shows hikers climbing down the final chute. Once down the chute, head NE up another slope to the ridgeline and follow it to the peak. Photo 7 shows the antennas at the peak.

To Descend: Retrace your steps, following the path back to the saddle. From the saddle, climb to the ridgeline and follow it. Remember to watch for the burned area. Head west (right) down the ridgeline to your car, which should be visible from the ridgeline.

Photo 4

Photo 5

Photo 6

Photo 7

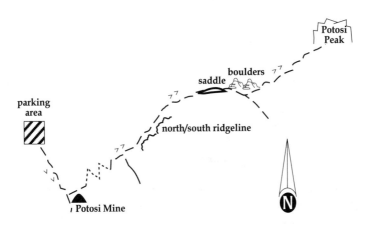

◆ ◆ ◆

Gass Peak

Hike: Gass Peak — up and back
Trailhead: Along Gass Peak Road — not marked
Distance: 8 miles — round trip
Elevation gain: 2,025 feet
Elevation peak: 6,943 feet
Time: 4 to 5 hours
Difficulty: 3
Danger level: 2
How easy to follow: 3
Children: no
Topo map: Gass Peak, NEV

Directions: Take U.S. 95 approximately 15 miles past the Santa Fe Hotel and Casino and turn right onto the signed "Desert National Wildlife Range Road." Drive about 4 miles along this gravel road, then stop and sign the register at the Desert National Wildlife Range (Corn Creek Field Station). This unmanned station has bathrooms, running water, and brochures. Continue up the road and turn SE (right) onto Mormon Well Road. At 4.5 miles turn south (right) onto the signed Gass Peak Road. Drive approximately 8.5 miles, turn right, and park at the entrance to a service road with a sign that reads, "Service Road—Unauthorized Entry Prohibited." A four-wheel drive is recommended.

Overview: The **route** travels the service road, then follows a series of connecting ridgelines to the peak.

Comments: The large antenna installed on the top of Gass Peak is an excellent landmark. The views of Las Vegas from the peak are unique and among the best in the whole area. This hike can be done as a fitness hike; a good time to the peak is less than two hours.

Gass Peak

Photo 1

The Hike: Hike up the service road. (See Photo 1.) When it forks, go left and continue a half-mile until the road ends near a Joshua tree. From this point until you reach the peak, you'll hike along various ridgelines. Much of the hike is cross-country, though at times you'll follow faint paths.

Head south (200 degrees) up the slope that starts near the Joshua tree. Continue south up three small rises that are separated by short stretches of level terrain. Just beyond the third rise, the ridgeline swings left and heads SE (150 degrees) toward the main ridgeline that will take you to Gass Peak. You can see the peak at this point. There's a faint path to follow, and the grade is moderate.

Soon a perpendicular ridgeline appears. Hike SE to get to it, then go SW (right) along the perpendicular ridgeline. To the east, you'll see part of Interstate 15. Photo 2 was taken along this ridgeline and shows the route to the peak.

Once you're on the path (see Photo 2), Gass Peak is to your right. Follow the path up the steep slope. If you lose the path, just keep hiking SE to the top of the slope. At the top, you're rewarded with 60 yards of flat terrain before trekking up another

Gass Peak

Photo 2

steep slope. When you've conquered the second slope, you'll be able to see Las Vegas. Head SW (240 degrees) along this ridgeline toward the ridge that takes you to Gass Peak.

Finally you're on the ridge that travels to the peak. Trudge 210 degrees up the steep ridgeline until it flattens out. The antenna briefly comes into view before disappearing behind the final slope. A wall of limestone, just before the peak, splits the terrain into two levels. Hike along the top of the limestone wall. At this point the antenna is in sight, and you're less than 100 yards from the peak.

Be sure to sign the register that sits in the cairn. There's an array of communication equipment, in addition to the antenna, at the peak. You'll enjoy terrific views of Mt. Charleston to the west and Las Vegas to the south. The dirt road cutting across the desert toward Gass Peak is Jones Boulevard, which serves as a trailhead for a different route to the peak.

To Descend: Retrace your steps. As you descend, use the service road as a landmark.

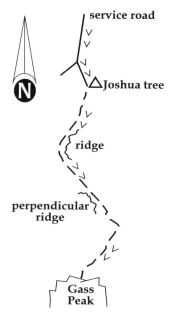

◆ ◆ ◆

Hayford Peak

Hike: Hayford Peak — up and back
Trailhead: End of Hidden Forest Road — not marked
Distance: 15 miles — round trip
Elevation gain: 4,100 feet
Elevation peak: 9,912 feet
Time: 9 to 10 hours
Difficulty: 5
Danger level: 2
How easy to follow: 5
Children: no
Topo map: Hayford Peak, NEV and Sheep Peak, NEV

Directions: Take U.S. 95 approximately 15 miles past the Santa Fe Hotel and Casino and turn right onto the signed "Desert National Wildlife Range Road." Drive about 4 miles along this gravel road, then stop and sign the register at the Desert National Wildlife Range (Corn Creek Field Station). This unmanned station has bathrooms, running water, and brochures. Continue up the road and make a left onto the signed Alamo Road. Drive 15 miles and turn right onto the signed Hidden Forest Road, which ends in 3.5 miles at a locked gate. A four-wheel-drive vehicle is recommended.

Overview: Hike east along a gravel **trail** to Hidden Forest cabin. From there, the **route** follows a drainage to a cross-country trek to the western ridgeline. Hike the ridgeline to the peak.

Comments: Hayford Peak is the highest point in the Sheep Mountain Range. Keep your eyes open to spot desert bighorn sheep; they're more prevalent here than anywhere else in the world. You can stop and rest at the log cabin before hiking the final 2.5 miles to

Photo 1

Hayford Peak, which is easily recognized by its array of communication equipment. Due to the relatively low starting elevation (5,812 feet), this hike is best done in the fall or spring.

The Hike: The unmarked trail begins at the iron gate. The trail, which is actually a gravel road that later turns into a wash, heads east up Deadman's Canyon. Although the incline remains slight throughout the 5 miles to the log cabin, hiking in gravel is strenuous. The first part of the 5 miles weaves through the 100-foot walls of Deadman's Canyon. The terrain is typical high desert. When you come to a series of forks, always take the left forks, which have less gravel. Photo 1 shows the first of many forks. Remember that you're in a canyon following a wash that divides and joins several times, so you can't veer too far off course.

Around the 4-mile point, the high desert terrain gives way to mountain terrain. Ponderosa pines tower above the trail. The wash disappears and the trail turns into an abandoned road. The direction changes to NE, but the incline remains slight. When the trail passes two huge logs, look left to see a rock

Photo 2

Photo 3

arch. The log cabin lies just beyond the logs.

The cabin is a perfect place to take a break. The picnic tables, fire pit, and seasonal running water from a pipe enable you to relax in a peaceful setting. Be sure to sign the register inside the cabin. This might be the turnaround point for some, since the hike from here to the peak becomes very strenuous.

Are you ready? Continue north on the same abandoned road; it lies just west (left) of the cabin. When the road turns into a faint path, it drops into a small drainage. You'll pass two large logs as you follow the drainage north toward Hayford Peak. The incline increases as the faint path travels up the right side of the drainage. When the drainage divides, go north into the left fork. At this point you'll get your first glimpse of Hayford Peak. (See Photo 2.) From here, head NW and parallel a deep drainage that lies to your right. Eventually, you'll see the western ridgeline to the NW. Hike NW up the steep slope to the ridgeline. Once on the ridgeline, follow a faint path that leads to the peak. If you lose the path, continue along the ridgeline and you'll eventually find it again. Along most of the ridgeline the peak is in sight, making your direction of travel obvious. Photo 3 was taken from the ridgeline.

Outcroppings

Photo 4

When you come to a saddle, rest for a moment before starting up the steep slope. At the top of the slope, the terrain levels and the hiking is easier. As you approach the base of the peak, the path goes down into another saddle. Notice the craggy outcroppings in Photo 4. You want to stay below and left of them before making your final ascent to the peak. Follow the faint path as it cuts its way up the west (left) side of the mountain. Continue on the path, pass the outcroppings, then look up to the right. Where you see the terrain start to level off above, scramble up to that point. Depending on your location along the level terrain, you might be able to see the antennas on the peak (to your left). Hike 150 yards or less to the peak.

You made it! Reflecting panels, antennas, and a storage shed share the peak with you. Write your name in the sign-in book that sits in the cairn. When you start your descent, make sure to descend the correct ridgeline. It's SW about 210 degrees.

To Descend: Retrace your steps along the ridgeline. An option for experienced hikers is to find the drainage nestled between the west and east ridgelines and follow it back to the cabin. The overall direction is south. All the various drainages lead back to the cabin, which makes the route-finding easier. Descending the drainage is about a half-mile shorter than descending along the ridge.

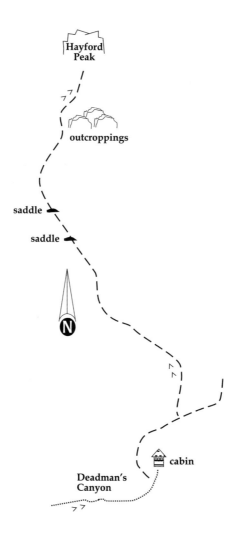

♦ GLOSSARY ♦

bouldering: Using hands and feet to climb over, around, or down large boulders. Most bouldering routes are in the canyons of Red Rock.

buttress: A large flat portion of rock that stands out from a wall behind it.

cairn: A pile of rocks used to mark a path or route.

canyon: A deep narrow valley with high steep sides.

catch basin: A depression in sandstone rock where water collects.

chimney: A steep narrow chute with parallel walls.

chute: A steep, well-worn passage where debris often funnels down from a mountain. A chute is larger than a crack but smaller than a gully.

closed loop: A trail or path that makes a complete circle.

conglomerate: A rock composed of many types of pebbles and minerals.

crack: A fracture in a rock; varies in size.

crag: A sandstone wall scaled by technical climbers.

cryptobiotic soil: A fragile type of soil found near Lake Mead. Do not walk on it.

declination: The angle that a freely turning magnetic needle makes with the imaginary line that points true north.

face: The steep side of a mountain.

fall: A normally dry place that becomes a waterfall when it rains or snows. A dry fall is a class II or higher climb.

gully: A broad, low-angled depression that runs vertically down the side of a mountain.

malachite: A mineral that is a green carbonate of copper.

narrows: A tight passageway in a wash; formed by wind and water erosion over thousands of years.

open loop: A trail or path that makes an incomplete circle. The trailhead and the trail's end are in different locations.

pass: An obvious cleft or break in a ridgeline where it is possible to cross.

path: A non-maintained pathway that's more difficult to follow than a trail, but easier to follow than a route. Some paths are former trails that have become overgrown or faded.

pullout: A place to park along a paved road. A pullout is either paved or made of gravel or dirt.

ramp: An inclined sandstone ledge.

ravine: A small, narrow, steep-sided valley that's larger than a gully but smaller than a canyon.

rock scrambling: Class II and Class III climbing up and over rock without the use of ropes.

route: A trek that's hiked by using landmarks. There are no marked paths or trails to follow.

saddle: A low point between two peaks, ridgelines, or high points.

sandstone: Porous rock made of sand; found at Red Rock.

scree: An accumulation of small rocks found on a slope.

slope: A very low-angled face of a mountain.

summit: The peak of a mountain.

suzan: A line of small rocks that marks the way; used as a landmark when the terrain is too steep to make a cairn.

switchback: The zigzag pattern in a trail or path that makes it easier to go up the side of a mountain.

talus: Loose rock and gravel on a slope.

tank: A place larger than a catch basin where water gathers after a rainstorm. Calico Tank is the best example.

topo map: A map showing the details of the contour of the land by means of lines and symbols.

trail: A well-maintained pathway that's easy to follow.

trailhead: The starting point of a trail, path, or route.

vista: A distant view from a high point or peak.

About the Author

Branch Whitney first visited the mountains (Rockies) at the age of seven and knew immediately that he wanted to climb them. Within two weeks of moving to Las Vegas in 1983, he bagged Mt. Charleston. Since then, he's logged more than 2,000 miles hiking the trails, paths, and routes surrounding Las Vegas. These days, he stays busy leading hikes for the Sierra Club and the Las Vegas Mountaineer's Club, and also maintaining his web site. Anyone who would like to share ideas, tips, favorite hikes, or noteworthy experiences on the trails of Southern Nevada can contact Branch at www.hikinglasvegas.com or at the address below.

Branch Whitney
c/o Huntington Press ·
3687 South Procyon Avenue
Las Vegas, Nevada 89103
e-mail: books@huntingtonpress.com

About Huntington Press

Huntington Press is a specialty publisher of gambling- and Las Vegas-related books and periodicals, including the award-winning consumer newsletter, *Anthony Curtis' Las Vegas Advisor*. To receive a copy of the Huntington Press catalog, call **1-800-244-2224** or write to the address below.

Huntington Press
3687 South Procyon Avenue
Las Vegas, Nevada 89103

Look for these Huntington Press books at your local bookstore

***No Limit—The Rise and Fall of Bob Stupak and Las Vegas'
Stratosphere Tower*** by John L. Smith

A penetrating look at Bob Stupak, controversial casino owner and builder of the Stratosphere Tower. Between his early days as the son of a notorious Pittsburgh gambler and the grand opening of the Stratosphere, Stupak raced motorcycles, hustled discount coupons, ran Vegas World, made a $1 million winning Super Bowl bet, and much more. Author John L. Smith is a featured columnist for the *Las Vegas Review-Journal*.

298 pages, hardcover, $21.95 (ISBN #0-929712-18-8)

On the Boulevard—The Best of John L. Smith by John L. Smith

John L. Smith has written more than 2,000 columns that have appeared in the *Las Vegas Review-Journal*. *On the Boulevard* brings together the best of them, providing singular insight into the fast, fluid, and often funny town that Smith has chronicled for the past 15 years.

315 pages, softcover, $12.95 (ISBN #0-929712-69-2)

Madam—Chronicles of a Nevada Cathouse by Lora Shaner

Have you ever wondered what really happens inside a Nevada brothel? Former madam Lora Shaner tells all in *Madam—Chronicles of a Nevada Cathouse*. This no-holds-barred exposé takes you behind the closed doors of Sheri's Ranch, the legal brothel where Shaner worked. You'll be introduced to the women who sell sex—and the men who buy it. Featured in *Penthouse* magazine.

305 pages, hardcover, $24.95 (ISBN #0-929712-57-9)

***Fly on the Wall—Recollections of Las Vegas' Good Old,
Bad Old Days*** by Dick Odessky

Read about Bugsy Siegel, Benny Binion, Mo Dalitz, Jackie Gaughn, and Lefty Rosenthal, to name just a few, in this fascinating account of the Las Vegas of the '40s, '50s, and '60s. Author Dick Odessky was the proverbial "fly on the wall" during the glamour years of Sin City. He came to Las Vegas in the early '50s as a newspaper reporter and quickly found himself in the company of powerful politicians, famous entertainers, and notorious gangsters. An informative read, packed with never-before-told stories.

245 pages, hardcover, $21.95 (ISBN #0-929712-61-7)

***The First 100—Portraits of the Men and Women Who
Shaped Las Vegas*** edited by A.D. Hopkins and K.J. Evans

A.D. Hopkins and K.J. Evans of the *Las Vegas Review-Journal* bring to life the incredible men and women who ushered Las Vegas to the forefront of popular culture. The 100 profiles, punctuated by hundreds of black-and-white photographs, in this heirloom-quality volume bring the history of Las Vegas to life in a way that no other book has before.

288 pages, hardcover, $34.95 (ISBN #0-929712-66-8)

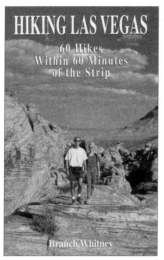